HOW TO BE A CHRISTIAN

IN A BRAVE NEW WORLD

Books by Joni Eareckson Tada

All God's Children: Ministry with Disabled Persons
(with Gene Newman)

Barrier-Free Friendships: Bridging the Distance Between You
and Friends with Disabilities (with Steve Jensen)

Diamonds in the Dust: 366 Sparkling Devotions

The God I Love

Heaven: Your Real Home

Heaven: Devotional Edition

Joni

The Life and Death Dilemma: Suicide, Euthanasia, Suffering, Mercy

More Precious Than Silver: 366 Daily Devotional Readings

A Step Further (with Steven Estes)

When God Weeps: Why Our Sufferings Matter to the Almighty
(with Steven Estes)

When Is It Right to Die?

JONI EARECKSON TADA
& NIGEL M. DE S. CAMERON

HOW TO BE A CHRISTIAN
IN A BRAVE NEW WORLD

ZONDERVAN™

GRAND RAPIDS, MICHIGAN 49530 USA

ZONDERVAN.COM/
AUTHORTRACKER

ZONDERVAN™

How to Be a Christian in a Brave New World
Copyright © 2006 by Joni Eareckson Tada and Nigel M. de S. Cameron

Requests for information should be addressed to:
Zondervan, *Grand Rapids, Michigan 49530*

Library of Congress Cataloging-in-Publication Data

Tada, Joni Eareckson.
    How to be a Christian in a brave new world / Joni Eareckson Tada,
Nigel M. de S. Cameron.
        p. cm.
    Includes bibliographical references and index.
    ISBN-13: 978-0-310-25939-8
    ISBN-10: 0-310-25939-8
    1. Christian life. 2. Bioethics—Religious aspects—Christianity. 3. Medical ethics—
Religious aspects—Christianity. 4. Christian ethics. I. Cameron, Nigel M. de S. II. Title.
    BV4501.3.T32   2006
    241'.6429—dc22
                                                                                    2005030455

Published in association with the literary agency of Wolgemuth & Associates, Inc.

Interior design by Beth Shagene

Printed in the United States of America

06 07 08 09 10 11 12 • 22 21 20 19 18 17 16 15 14 13 12 11 10 9 8 7 6 5 4 3 2

To George W. Bush,
Forty-third President of the United States,
defender of the dignity of human life;
with deep respect and in appreciation

CONTENTS

As the discoveries of modern science create tremendous hope, they also lay vast ethical minefields. As the genius of science extends the horizons of what we can do, we increasingly confront complex questions about what we should do. We have arrived at that brave new world that seemed so distant in 1932, when Aldous Huxley wrote about human beings created in test tubes in what he called a "hatchery."

GEORGE W. BUSH

A Little Background

Joni Eareckson Tada

I've never been one for high-minded oratory. At the University of Maryland, I'd lean on my elbow in Philosophy 101 and fight off sleep whenever my professor droned in standard lecture-hall monotone. When dissertations became long-winded or delivered in the language of manuals or big textbooks, my mind would head for the college cafeteria.

"Don't give me the *War and Peace* version, just answer my questions." Seriously now, did anybody really *care* that "I think, therefore I am"? A system of values? Moral absolutes? Wasn't right just, well … right? Wasn't wrong as easy to discern as night and day? Whether ethics were situational or rigid was of little use to me. Wasn't it a fact that in most situations, all you needed to do was apply a little common sense? Like: would it land you in jail? Does it hurt anybody? Would the pope disapprove?

I refused to take the time or mental energy to search out answers to really sticky ethical questions. If people smarter than I was couldn't speak plainly or point me in the right direction, then I walked away thinking no meaningful answer existed. I took the casual approach—I skirted along the edge of an ethical issue only to catch an occasional idea that buzzed or resonated.

We do it all the time. If we're not guilty of a lazy mental attitude, maybe we're just afraid of tough questions. Or frightened of the answers—answers that demand that we change.

But somewhere along the line, our thinking begins to shift.

For me, it happened after a diving accident left me permanently paralyzed and drowning in despair; after a cancerous tumor ate away my five-year-old niece's brain; and after a series of strokes tangled my ninety-year-old father in a web of tubes and machines. Somewhere in

those family tragedies, my thinking shifted. Ethics were no longer confined to classroom discussion; moral judgments now had flesh-and-blood
reality. I had to find an honest-to-goodness reason why quadriplegics
like me shouldn't kill themselves ... why we shouldn't "mercifully" cut
short my niece's suffering ... and what we should do about all those
tubes and machines.

Suddenly I was digging for answers. Books on ethics became my
nighttime reading companions. Dinnertime conversations spilled into
lively debates about right and wrong. Bible studies evolved into late-
night wrestling matches, trying to pin the Word of God to every weird
medical scenario. What *does* the Bible say if the agony of a disease is too
great to bear? What *is* the difference between treatment that sustains
life and that which does nothing more than delay death? When is it *okay*
to remove the plugs and let your daddy die?

I flipped furiously through the Bible until I landed on James 1:5: "If
any of you lacks wisdom, he should ask God ... and it will be given to
him." I knew I was thin on wisdom; I lacked "the power of judging the
soundest course of action based on knowledge and experience." I also
knew, from the Bible, that I could gain an ability to *discern*. Eventually, after much soul-searching and fact-finding, my family was able to
apply God's wisdom to my father's and niece's situation. I also gained a
personal wisdom — I began to embrace all the life God wanted to give me,
even if it meant living in a wheelchair without use of my hands or legs.

That's when things heated up. I realized I could help other people who
were sinking into despair: people with Lou Gehrig's disease ... young
men paralyzed from spinal cord injuries and living in nursing homes
... and teenagers with cerebral palsy sitting on the sidelines, watching their classmates date and drive cars. I began sharing with them
what I'd learned from God's Word. Before long, I was writing letters
to editors and articles for national magazines, asserting that people
are not "better off dead than disabled." I was speaking with politicians
and advocates, rallying a coalition to defeat a physician-assisted suicide
initiative in my state. I was arguing against the abortion of unborn
handicapped infants as a "disability prevention measure." I was serving
on the National Council on Disability under two US presidents, telling

legislators that their "fear of disability" should not provide the basis for making social policy.

These were deep waters. Cloudy and turbulent waters. As soon as we succeeded in damming one river of controversy, a new medical development opened up another stream of thought. What about experimenting on human embryos? How can we design better babies? Why not create clones to harvest their organs? Medical technology stormed ahead at hurricane speed, creating all sorts of complex situations that demanded answers. Before it had a chance to examine a moral compass, society found itself swept away into a brave new world.

Once again, I struggled in the midst of a raging torrent, seeking the higher ground of God's Word. I faced things I knew little about and had virtually no experience in. I sought safety in the abundance of counselors, as Proverbs told me to do. I went to experts who had already begun charting these uncharted waters. Counselors like John F. Kilner of the Center for Bioethics and Human Dignity; C. Ben Mitchell, associate professor of bioethics and contemporary culture at Trinity International University; and Dr. Christopher Hook, director of ethics education for the Mayo Graduate School of Medicine.

One of my favorite mentors has been Dr. Nigel M. de S. Cameron, former dean of the Wilberforce Forum, who also has served as provost and distinguished professor of theology and culture at Trinity International University/Trinity Evangelical Divinity School. This is not the sort of fellow with whom I normally share a pizza, but Nigel has been an invaluable advisor in helping me to navigate the bizarre new world of biotechnology and the questions it raises about cloning, assisted suicide, infertility treatments, and strange new methods of medical research.

Just as with Daddy and my cancer-ridden niece, as well as my own quadriplegia, we *urgently* need answers. What do I say to the pair of female quadriplegics in California who are raising funds to promote research that uses human embryos? How do I reply to the man with multiple sclerosis who believes he can do whatever he wants with his body, even if it means three grams of phenobarbital in his veins to end his suffering? What do I tell my neighbor, a single woman who wants to buy sperm over the Internet? Or, closer to home, what do I tell my friend who is using in vitro technology to ensure her child avoids substandard health? (What in the world could possibly be wrong with a mother wanting a healthy baby?)

It's not so much a brave new world as a strange one. And like me, you need answers; you need wisdom; you need to know the soundest course of action when confronted by complex biotechnological issues. I promise, if you take the time and mental energy to seriously weigh the issues in this book, you'll find no high-minded oratory. I promise: no dissertations delivered in the language of manuals or big textbooks. As you turn each page, we won't skirt the edge of an issue; Dr. Nigel Cameron and I will help you understand the complexities, judge the soundest course of action, and gain discernment. We'll point you to the higher ground of God's Word and show you *How to Be a Christian in a Brave New World.*

For God calls *you* to be the brave one in this strange new world.

HOW I GOT HERE

Nigel M. de S. Cameron

When I find myself talking in churches and colleges about the questions discussed in this book, I often start by giving a little of my background. That's partly because after nearly fifteen years in the US, I still sound very much like a Brit! It helps to get the audience used to your accent before you really get going. I also think that telling how I got here may help some of *you* get here too, because that's really what I want.

In school I had no plans to get into bioethics. I planned for a career in pastoral ministry, though politics had always interested me. I was a pro-life Christian and had actually arranged in my homeland for the premiere of the movie series by Francis Schaeffer and C. Everett Koop, *Whatever Happened to the Human Race*—a work that had a profound impact on the church in the late 1970s, waking up many believers to the importance of abortion and euthanasia. But I became concerned that Christians seemed to have no appetite to move beyond abortion. Even to get them interested in euthanasia was a stretch. And all the time, hot new issues kept coming down the pike. The new stuff got left for the academics who had founded "bioethics" and set its secular terms. I went to some of their conferences and found hardly a soul there who thought as I did.

So back in the early 1980s I got together with some friends and started a journal called *Ethics and Medicine*. We ran some conferences on test-tube babies and euthanasia and other issues, and we published books. We worked with physicians, nurses, philosophers, theologians, and lawyers to grapple with the new questions and the old ones that an increasingly secular society forced on us. We kept asking ourselves: How should Christians think about these things? And what can we do? I thought that once we got going, this movement would grow huge. Every believer would "get it" and schools, parachurch ministries, and wealthy donors would all want to get in on the act. Christians would wake up and realize two facts.

First, they would realize that the biotech agenda is the biggest thing on the face of the planet, stretching from killing in the womb to killing outside the womb, and then on to even more sinister things that lead to reshaping human nature itself.

Second, they would realize that we are here "for such a time as this." Christians understand what being human means – God tells us he has made us in his image. So now is the time for us to stand up, be counted, and make all the difference as the world struggles with new technologies and old temptations.

For some reason, things have not turned out quite as I had expected.

Many Christians really don't seem to care. Others may say they care but don't like to *think* as Christians (even though they may be very good at thinking in their jobs and schools). Whatever the reason, a quarter century later we have not got much closer to making the connections. Secularists dominate the bio discussions. Few pastors bother to teach their congregations about these things – or even learn about them. When I came to Trinity Evangelical Divinity School in 1991, I was astonished to discover that not one evangelical school in the US had a grad program in bioethics – or even an undergrad program for their premeds! We soon changed that.

Trinity started a bioethics MA, and at the undergraduate level we began a minor in bioethics. We invited a dozen Christians from around the nation to come to campus and talk strategy – including C. Ben Mitchell and John F. Kilner, who have since become close colleagues and friends. Out of that meeting we started the Center for Bioethics and Human Dignity, which has since spawned a national network through the Center for Bioethics and Culture. Then, when I left Trinity in the late 1990s and began to spend some of my time working with Charles W. Colson in Washington, DC, we started the Council for Biotechnology Policy as an affiliate of Chuck's Wilberforce Forum.

While most Christians just don't "get it," someone who has always grasped what is going on is Joni Eareckson Tada. Just weeks after my family moved to the States in 1991, Joni and I began to get to know each other. She was working on her powerful book on euthanasia, *When Is It Right to Die?* From the beginning she has remained in the forefront of sane, well-informed, yet passionate defense of human life. With cloning and embryo stem cell research at the top of the public agenda, she has been uniquely qualified to testify to the integrity of human life and the need for ethical science. And she has done so with grace and intelligence, all the way from the extensive speaking ministry she tirelessly pursues to the center point of our national debates – *Larry King Live.* Back in 2002, when President Bush finished his inspiring speech against cloning and the abuse of technology, I watched him step down from the podium and give her a hug.

So come join us as we explore how we can be Christians in the brave new world, and then join us in the task of serving God in the special challenges of the twenty-first century.

That's why he put us here.

PART ONE

The Brave New World

In 1932, English writer Aldous Huxley wrote one of the most famous books of all time, with the strange title *Brave New World*. The title is a quote from Shakespeare's play *The Tempest* and suggests both the boldness and the folly of something that looks like a utopia (paradise) even though it much more closely approaches the opposite.

Eleven years later, C. S. Lewis wrote a short essay that some people consider the most important thing he ever did. With incredible insight, his work *The Abolition of Man* looked ahead to the technologies of the twenty-first century and warned that a world that uncritically accepts the wonders of biotech will eventually devastate human dignity.

Thus the secular Huxley and the Christian Lewis set the stage for the challenges of the twenty-first century. Some of these challenges still await us; many already are with us. Christians need to be prepared so they can be "salt and light" in the time and place where God has placed them.

Human beings are unique because God made us "in his image," as the Bible makes so clear in Genesis 1 and Psalm 8. Reminding ourselves of what it means to be made in God's image is the starting point for understanding what medicine, science, and technology should be used for — and what they should not.

In the last chapter of this section, we need to hear the long-forgotten story of what happened a hundred years ago, when Americans discovered "eugenics" — the desire for "good genes" at all costs — before the Nazis ever came to power in Germany and took those same ideas to their logical conclusion. We need to remember, because eugenics is making a comeback.

CHAPTER 1

STARTING OUT

LARRY

On a misty evening in September 2002, Larry drove his eighteen-wheeler into a gas station in a small Arizona town. He hopped out of the cab, started filling his tank, and then walked along the flatbed to check the restraining bands on his huge load of pipes. That's when it happened. A band snapped. Then another. Before he could run, the pipes came crashing down, smothering him under a massive pile. Larry tried to push the large metal cylinders away but couldn't. They not only crushed his lungs and collarbone but his spinal cord. He lay bruised, barely breathing, and unable to move.

Three months later, he was sitting in a wheelchair, staring out the window of a nursing home.

I heard about Larry when his aunt wrote to ask if I would send him one of my books. She explained that he's now paralyzed from the neck down and trying his best to adjust to his wheelchair, including life in an institution. He's twenty-eight years old, single, and can't speak because of the big ventilator in his neck. Larry, she said, is deeply depressed.

I wasted no time in tracking Larry down. When I learned he had a website, I browsed through a handful of emails written by his friends. Most of them came from his beer-drinking buddies and described all the parties he was missing. It was enough to push me further to hunt up Larry's mother. I got her on the phone.

"He's a good boy," she lamented. "And this is all so horrible ... he wishes he weren't so paralyzed so he could end his life. He's desperate to kill himself."

Her words made me shiver. I can understand a desire to kill oneself. I'm a quadriplegic; I understand everything he's going through, from bed baths to bowel programs, from pressure sores to the painful stares

from others. Thirty-eight years ago when I broke my neck, I saw no reason to go on either. Back then, I wrenched my neck violently on my pillow at night, hoping to break it at a higher level. I looked forward to the day I would gain enough movement to drive a power wheelchair; then I could drive myself off a curb and into traffic. Only when I realized that I might become brain injured did I drop the idea.

I'll bet Larry feels the same way. I'll bet that at night he fights off the claustrophobia, carefully plotting ways he can quietly end his life. If he smokes, I know what he's thinking when he draws on his cigarette, holding the smoke in his lungs: *Maybe this way I'll get lung cancer. Yeah, that's a quiet way—and a sure way—to end my life.*

Despair that deep simply devastates.

Yet today, things are worse for him than they were for me thirty-seven years ago. Three-and-a-half decades ago, society didn't so quickly assume that a severely injured person makes a rational choice if he ends his life. Fewer doctors bought into the premise, "You're better off dead than disabled." No Jack Kevorkians offered to aid me in my death wish; compassion was still something other than three grams of phenobarbital in the veins. Now, in 2005, a ventilator for a severely injured person might be termed "futile care." In fact, Larry's institution probably has in place futile care policies; that is, directives that allow doctors to overrule a family's wishes for treatment.

Who would ever have thought we would one day call care *futile*?

Larry doesn't care about any of that. He thinks his life *is* futile. He's convinced he would be better off dead than disabled. He would say, "What I do with my life is none of your business. I'm entitled to exercise my independence. It's fundamental to what this country is all about. And if they don't soon find a cure for people like me, then I'm out of here!"

This man's hell-bent on getting cured—and if not that, then killed.

I took a deep breath and decided to email Larry at his website. I then made a mental list of things I wanted to send him, support I wanted to give, and answers I wanted to help him find—even new info on possible cures for spinal cord injury. Most of all, I prayed, *Oh, Lord, show me how to be a Christian to this man ... and please give wisdom.*

Larry, bless his heart, needs wisdom too ...

BROOKE

Brooke and Travis are the kind of couple you'd run into at Starbucks on a Saturday afternoon. They'd be in their jogging outfits, slouched on a comfortable couch in the corner, sipping lattes and flipping through the *LA Times*. Travis works in the movie industry as a computer animation consultant, while Brooke enjoys her supervisor job at Kinko's. They lease a BMW, hold season tickets to the LA Lakers, live in a spacious house in the west end of the San Fernando Valley, and own the latest dog of fashion, a Jack Russell terrier. They have two little girls, one in preschool, the other into Scottish dancing.

Brooke and Travis are happy.

Brooke just celebrated her thirty-fifth birthday—in style. They threw a big party in their large home, and after dinner, she received more than her fair share of gag gifts and you're-not-getting-older-but-better cards. The cards and gifts bothered her a little. This was the first birthday she ever experienced that nagging fear of aging. She knows her biological clock is winding down, and she very much wants to have another child. There's only one problem.

Travis wants their next—and last—child to be a boy, no ifs, ands, or buts. "Honey, I love our little girls—but three in a row?" He gave a wry smile and rubbed his head. "I'm just not *there*."

Brooke feels the pressure—not just from age but from her own dreams and desires as well as her husband's expectations. Travis doesn't mind going to their daughter's Scottish dance recitals, nor does he mind the bills from Laura Ashley. It's just, well ... he dreams of the day he can take a son of his fly-fishing. Although her husband doesn't talk about it much, Brooke knows the many factors in the mix: their bank account, the limits on how many children they want, and most of all, Travis's preferences. And if you pressed Brooke, she probably would say the same. If they are going to have another child, they want it to be a boy.

Not long ago while at the dentist's office, Brooke read an article in a medical journal about "balancing your family." It sounded innocent enough, so she read on. She learned of a couple who, in the privacy of their own home, collected and then overnight-mailed sperm samples to an infertility clinic. After a day or two, they received a rapid turnaround of that sample, along with complete instructions on how to have a baby of their own choosing. The story intrigued Brooke but also made her feel a little uneasy. It seemed so *unnatural*—choosing the sex of your baby? But then she read of couple after couple who felt delighted with this new technology and thrilled to be able to have the chance to plan their families. One mother in the article effused, "We've always wanted a boy. What could be more natural than having a son along with all our daughters?"

That got the wheels in Brooke's head turning.

Later that evening she and her husband pored over the magazine. They had heard of the term "gender selection" before, but this procedure somehow didn't seem high tech or "medical." It simply allowed a couple to sort through sperm to help them choose the sex of their children and better balance their family. They liked that term, "family balance"—such a reasonable ring to it. That night as they lay in bed, Brooke and Travis decided this gave an answer to their deepest longings. This was their dream come true, the answer to their prayers. Brooke would have another baby ... and Travis would have a son. No ifs, ands, or buts about it.

The next day, Brooke had lunch with her girlfriend from church. She hadn't planned to discuss the magazine article, but she couldn't conceal her excitement. After she told her friend about the new service provided by the infertility clinic, she leaned over her coffee and said in a loud whisper, "It's so *easy.* Travis is calling them today!"

Had you been there, you would have seen the shock on the face of her friend. You would have sensed the awkward pause. But in the next moment, you too might have flipped open the magazine and read the stories of the families and happy parents. The shock would quickly soften. You'd comment that if the technology is available, why not? You might even find yourself using the lingo: "family balancing."

But somewhere that night, in that gray time of half sleep, when the Spirit brings to mind the conversations of the day, you might stop and think ... *really* think about what it means to select the sex of a child.

And then you'd wonder, *Lord, what do you think? What would you have me do?*

THE SCIENTIST

It's not often I see a world-renowned scientist shake his head in near dismay over his own research, but that day I witnessed it. The short news interview with him was telling.

He'd been serving for years as a specialist in the field of genetic screening. For much of that time, fertility clinics had been sending him human embryos for his careful scrutiny. This specialist, one of the few in the country who can "break down" an embryo's DNA and immediately spot an abnormality, actually pioneered the process. For a long time he's felt satisfied with his work, knowing he was "screening" human embryos that carried defective or missing genes. This meant—he thought—fulfilled and happy parents who fully expected healthy children.

That's what he thought.

But recently things have changed. Fertility clinics are beginning to send him special requests along with the embryo samples. No longer do they ask him to screen for diseases and deformities. Now they ask him to screen for the genes that determine whether the child will be a male or a female. They ask him to select embryos that will result in blue-eyed or brown-eyed children. He fears the day they will ask him to genetically screen out children with unacceptable IQs.

And he knows that day is approaching fast.

"I see it coming . . . sooner than we think. And *that's* an expert's opinion," he said in a somber tone.

As the news interview concluded, I had mixed feelings. I could tell from the look on this specialist's face that he felt conflicted, even sad. Yet I felt sadder that he seemed totally oblivious of his role in the snowballing scenario. Didn't he realize his pioneering technique would not only have potential for good but for evil as well? I'm sure his heart was in the right place when he invented the screening technique; but couldn't he imagine that other hearts would not be as altruistic? Jeremiah 17:9 would have told him so: "The heart is deceitful above all things." Evil has a way of wheedling its way into the best of intentions.

And speaking of evil, I had to shake my head not only at the genetic-screening-for-defects thing but also at the fertility clinics—the process of "selecting out" the so-called best embryos . . . the fittest ones . . . the ones parents "wanted," not to mention all the discarded embryos. The whole assisted-reproductive-technique business left a bitter taste in my mouth. I looked down at my own paralyzed legs — damaged goods, some might say — and I sensed a solidarity with those less-than-perfect human beings in the petri dish (and later, the dumpster).

Little wonder that scientist struggles with conflicted feelings! Some might call it guilt. Or some would point to Romans 2:14-15: "Even though they do not have the law ... the requirements of the law are written on their hearts, their consciences also bearing witness, and their thoughts now accusing ... them."

I don't have in mind merely the scientist's conscience. Or Larry and his mother's. Or the combined conscience of Brooke and Travis. The real point is, *our* conscience.

What of *our* sense of right and wrong? Would our scruples differ in the least from Larry's? Would we have decided differently from Brooke or Travis?

Some may not have the law, but we Christians do. And that law's requirements are written not just on our hearts but in our Bibles. We have answers to Larry's dilemma. We have something to say to Brooke and Travis. We can even instruct the scientist, for Psalm 119:99 tells us we "have more understanding than all [our] teachers: for [God's] testimonies are [our] meditation" (KJV).

We are Christians in a brave new world.

And we need not be afraid.

JONI

CHAPTER 2

THE BRAVE NEW WORLD

I couldn't help but feel nervous. The most famous interviewer in the world, Larry King, was about to interview me. I looked anxiously around the studio, so familiar to viewers of *Larry King Live* in more than 270 countries.

Well, I thought as the producer counted down, *this is it. I'm ready.*

I was well prepared. Two days earlier, one of the producers of *Larry King Live* had called to go over the sort of questions he'd ask. It both surprised and gladdened me that so many had to do with stem cell research—a topic I had been reading much on lately, especially since a spinal-cord-injured friend of mine was traveling to Lisbon, Portugal, to undergo an amazing spinal surgery that would use stem cells from her own nasal tissue. The success rate for the surgery was nothing short of miraculous. Former paraplegics were now walking—with braces, yes, but they were walking!

I had brushed up on my facts and felt ready to respond to Larry King's every question about the wonderful new treatments and therapies coming on the scene. From the number of questions the producer asked on the issue, I felt certain that most of the hour would focus on stem cell research. And, yes, I was especially ready to answer questions about Christopher Reeve, the paralyzed former movie star who had become a global advocate for using human cloning and embryonic stem cells to find cures.

About halfway through the interview ...

Larry King: "He [Reeve] thinks he's going to walk."

Joni: "That may very well happen, using incredible therapies ... using adult stem cell research. It is absolutely amazing what is happening. Dr. Carlos Lima in Lisbon, Portugal, has helped restore bladder and muscle control to people suffering from paralysis, using stem cells from their own nasal tissue!"

I fully expected Mr. King to say, "Oh, really? Tell us more!" After all, for the first time, the world had the chance to hear about the impossible and the miraculous. The world could learn about the never-before-heard-of medical success story of spinal-cord-injured people regaining feeling and movement in their bodies, using adult-tissue therapies. I prepared to explain that one paralyzed woman treated by Dr. Lima with her own olfactory tissue was about to appear before a Senate subcommittee to present videos of herself walking with braces!

I expected my answers to bowl over my host; perhaps he'd regain enough composure to pepper me for more details. And really, my announcement should have prompted a few follow-up questions, at least—but no. He didn't seem the least bit interested that paraplegics with spinal-cord injuries are on the verge of walking again. Instead, he took a different tack ...

Larry King: "Everyone says it will be faster if embryonic is also used. Nancy Reagan is going to campaign strongly for that."

I knew where he was going. It seemed clear Mr. King wanted to focus on the hotly emotional debate of embryonic stem cells. Didn't he hear what I just said about people paralyzed like me, like Christopher Reeve, already regaining movement and feeling? I tried to steer his line of questioning back onto adult stem cell successes ...

Joni: "Rather than focus on embryonic stem cells, I'm convinced we should channel what few and scarce resources there are into [adult] therapies which have the most promise, which are the most effective. Besides, stem cells from embryos can form tumors ... there's the problem with tissue rejection ... it's just not safe."

He shrugged off my comments and, instead, asserted that problems always happen in the beginning. "That's true," I acknowledged, trying again to get him to hear just how far adult-tissue research already has advanced, "but right now, incredible therapies are happening with our own stem cells, whether from dental pulp, nasal tissue, or bone-marrow tissues."

For the second time in two minutes, I had presented Larry King with the chance to provide his audience with a fascinating educational opportunity. Had he followed up—even skeptically demanding proof or examples—I could have told him about the forty-five diseases already being treated with adult-tissue therapies. I could have told him about human heart patients and people with Parkinson's who are enjoying amazing degrees of recovery. I could even have mentioned that sickle-cell anemia now has a 95 percent cure rate using stem cells from umbilical cord blood.

But my host did not allow a worldwide audience to hear any of this. Rather, Mr. King wound up the line of questioning with "What's the argument against using embryonic cells?" and an invitation for me to debate Christopher Reeve.

I don't know why, but the media believes that stem cell medical advancements count only if they come from human embryos. The media and many politicians are convinced that it is the religious extremists and ignorant ideologues who stand in the way. They insist that cures for cancers and diseases are within reach and that we must start funding embryonic stem cell research and cloning if those cures are to happen.

Well ... they are *already* happening.

It's the intellectuals, politicians, media, and many more who are shortsighted. Myopic. Faced with the facts, they refuse to see — blind by their own choosing. So is our secular society. Call them postmodern men or just plain dull, they stubbornly refuse to see, let alone come to the light.

If one passage from the Word of God best describes this strange new world in which we find ourselves, it's Matthew 13:13 - 15. Jesus makes a telling observation:

> *Though seeing, they do not see; though hearing, they do not hear or understand. In them is fulfilled the prophecy of Isaiah: "You will be ever hearing but never understanding; you will be ever seeing but never perceiving. For this people's heart has become calloused; they hardly hear with their ears, and they have closed their eyes. Otherwise they might see with their eyes, hear with their ears, and understand with their hearts."*

This is our brave new world, a world where people place their political views before the clear and present facts. It is a world where an irrational worldview sets the agenda.

And it's the world Jesus Christ bids us enter. He tells us in Matthew 5:13 – 16, "You are the salt of the earth. . . . You are the light of the world. A city on a hill cannot be hidden. Neither do people light a lamp and put it under a bowl. Instead they put it on its stand, and it gives light to everyone in the house. In the same way, let your light shine before men." And as you do, "they will see," it says in the last part of verse 16. Blind eyes, deaf ears, and calloused hearts will be changed.

But still, we need a clear ethical grid, something that will show us who we should be and what we should be doing in matters of science, health, and life. To what shall we look? The teachings of Scripture are the final court of appeals for ethics. Human reason and tradition may aid moral reflection, but the Bible serves as the bottom line. If we believe the Bible is indeed the Word of God, that it's the only reliable and infallible rule of faith, then it *must* be the highest authority for morals. By understanding the nature of God, man, good, and evil, the Bible provides a basic worldview within which we can grasp what we should believe in matters of science, health, and life.

In short, we must courageously move forward as a God-fearing people, possessing a Bible-based wisdom that will show us how to put our hands around everything from in vitro fertilization to the bizarre world of transhumanity. We need to see the brave new world as Jesus sees it. So . . .

> Get wisdom, get understanding; do not forget my words or swerve from them. Do not forsake wisdom, and she will protect you; love her, and she will watch over you. Wisdom is supreme; therefore get wisdom. Though it cost all you have, get understanding. Esteem her, and she will exalt you; embrace her, and she will honor you. (Proverbs 4:5 – 8)

JONI

With the dawn of the twenty-first century, we stand on the threshold of the brave new world. The debates about cloning and the use of embryos for stem cell research have awakened many of us to the special challenge of life in the third millennium. We know that there will be amazing advances in technology; we do not know whether our morals will keep up. Technology can serve wonderful purposes: to feed the starving, heal the sick, and spread the good news of Jesus. It also can give evil men and women (and, equally worrying, foolish men and women) enormous power over others and the world at large.

For a long time, thoughtful people have debated the merits of the two most influential books ever written about the future. They are alike in one respect: they offer visions of a world that has gone profoundly wrong.

Two Visions of the Future

George Orwell's *1984* sets out a vision of political oppression and control that foresees the triumph of technology in the service of dictatorship. Its theme: "Big Brother is watching you."

By contrast, Aldous Huxley's *Brave New World* offers a more subtle nightmare in which biotechnology has brought about a world where pain and suffering have been almost entirely alleviated — at the cost of everything that makes life worth living. It is hellish but, from the outside, looks like heaven.

In the closing years of the twentieth century, it became obvious which vision of the future was right. As Soviet Communism collapsed and the power of dictators crumbled around the world, scientists in an unknown lab in Scotland announced they had cloned Dolly the sheep — and the biotech revolution began. We have reason to feel grateful that Orwell seems to have been wrong. In the age of cloning, we have reason to be fearful that Huxley may have been right.

The challenge of human cloning confronts the world with a special opportunity. This is our chance to decide that human dignity always comes first, and that biotechnology — like all technology — must serve human beings and respect the dignity of those created in the image of God. The amazing benefits it promises always come mingled with threats.

The closing years of the twentieth century showed that George Orwell's totalitarian vision of a world under dictatorship did not represent the human future. It lies in our hands at the start of the twenty-first to ensure that, under God, Aldous Huxley is also proved wrong. But to

Excerpt from Aldous Huxley's *Brave New World*

A squat grey building of only thirty-four stories. Over the main entrance the words, CENTRAL LONDON HATCHERY AND CONDITIONING CENTRE, and, in a shield, the World State's motto, COMMUNITY, IDENTITY, STABILITY....

"And this," said the Director opening the door, "is the Fertilizing Room."

Bent over their instruments, three hundred Fertilizers were plunged, as the Director of Hatcheries and Conditioning entered the room, in the scarcely breathing silence, the absent-minded, soliloquizing hum or whistle, of absorbed concentration. A troop of newly arrived students, very young, pink and callow, followed nervously, rather abjectly, at the Director's heels. Each of them carried a notebook, in which, whenever the great man spoke, he desperately scribbled. Straight from the horse's mouth. It was a rare privilege. The D. H. C. for Central London always made a point of personally conducting his new students round the various departments.

"I shall begin at the beginning," said the D.H.C. and the more zealous students recorded his intention in their notebooks: *Begin at the beginning.* "These," he waved his hand, "are the incubators." And opening an insulated door he showed them racks upon racks of numbered test-tubes. "The week's supply of ova. Kept," he explained, "at blood heat; whereas the male gametes," and here he opened another door, "they have to be kept at thirty-five instead of thirty-seven. Full blood heat sterilizes." Rams wrapped in theremogene beget no lambs.

do so will require all our efforts. In our generation, the key decisions will be made to shape the world of tomorrow.

President George W. Bush made the point well. In April of 2002, he invited both of us, together with a group of Christian leaders and our secular allies, to the White House to hear him call for a comprehensive ban on human cloning. We won't easily forget his speech. Listen to these words:

Science has set before us decisions of immense consequence. We can pursue medical research with a clear sense of moral purpose or we can travel without an ethical compass into a world we could live to regret. Science now presses forward the issue of human cloning. How we answer the question of human cloning will place us on one path or the other.

As the president could clearly see, this is the benchmark debate of the biotech century.

We live in an age of technology, but technology is not new. Even the most primitive human societies used tools to make things and grow crops. The Industrial Revolution led to the slow replacement of an agricultural way of life with factories that manufactured first cloth, then later consumer products such as the automobile. Western countries have now moved into economies dominated by services, and information technology has begun to have a huge impact on how we lead our lives.

BIOTECHNOLOGY AND "DOMINION" OVER OURSELVES

While technology is not new, in this past generation technology has begun to change its focus. No longer is it aimed simply at the world around us. It has begun to turn its attention to us, ourselves, our human nature itself.

In 1978 we saw the birth of the world's first "test-tube baby," Louise Brown. Then, less than twenty years later, Dolly was born, the world's first clone. Technology now has a new, sinister twist. Technology is the story of our "conquest of nature." Now we have added human nature to "nature." The long story of our gaining "dominion" – right from the start one of our human tasks (Genesis 1:28 KJV) – has taken a fresh turn. We are working on getting "dominion" over ourselves. What does that mean? It's a question to which we will continually return.

But some things are becoming clear. When we formerly used the word *dominion* about people, we meant one of two things: dominion over other people, and dominion over ourselves. When we speak of dominion over other people, we mean politics and government, how we should rule ourselves in our villages and towns and nations, perhaps dominion over *other* nations. And the key to that question, recognized increasingly all over the world, is to treat people like people. That is basically what we mean by "human rights."

The idea of human rights comes down to us from the so-called Enlightenment of the eighteenth century, the period when some key intellectual leaders, for the first time in many hundreds of years, decided to look at human life apart from God – they cut him out of the picture and focused exclusively on humans. The history of the past two hundred years has largely been the story of our wrestling with that idea, and much of what is good and bad in the modern world came out of this fresh focus on what it means to be human.

On the plus side of the ledger, the civil rights movement of the 1960s, and "human rights" as a key idea in international law today, focus on human dignity, even if the statements do not explicitly recognize that our dignity finds its roots in God.

Sadly, there is more to be said on the negative side. The basic assumption of the modern world is that if you wish to believe in God, you should keep it to yourself; education, politics, the media, all operate as if he were not there.

The flowering of democracy and the idea that every person has rights owe everything to the impact of Christians and their Bible on Western culture. Our culture has been deeply influenced by the Bible's teaching that human beings – *all* human beings – are created in the image of God. This point is vital: *you must treat people as people.* That's the message that led to the end of slavery and the rise of the civil rights movement, and is also the message we still give to dictators and totalitarian states. It's the standard we in the West seek to live up to. God calls the nations to account for their treatment of his human creatures, whether in the killing fields of Cambodia or Rwanda. People must be treated like people.

It seems obvious, yet at the heart of current developments in biotech the distinction between *people* and *things* is getting increasingly blurred.

Second, we used to speak of "dominion" over ourselves in moral terms. Two generations ago a spate of books appeared with titles like "Self-mastery." The point was simple: To live well, humans need to exercise self-control. Christians ought to know much more about this than unbelievers because they understand the significance of sin. You need to have "dominion" over yourself if you are going to fulfill your potential and live a good life. It alarms many of us that today's children seem to be so undisciplined, because we know this will make it so much harder for them in later life to discipline themselves. This kind of "dominion" is also appropriate to human beings, since it treats them as people—as moral beings.

In light of this, we have to recognize that the threat posed by every one of the technologies we are about to examine is its tendency to blur the distinction between people and things—and, sometimes, to treat people as objects. This process has been called "commodification"—to treat someone as a commodity.

HUMANS AS COMMODITIES

Let's look at an example taken from a technology that has existed for half a century. Until recently, almost everyone agreed that the only ethical way to use human organs for transplants was for them to be "donated" as gifts, either from a live donor who could spare a kidney or some other part of the body, or from the relatives of someone who had died. Usually, the donor is dead by the time of the transplant. Most countries protect human organs from being bought and sold, although fees change hands to cover costs, and commercial organizations act as brokers—which underlines the "commodity" metaphor. Organs and other body tissue can easily be treated as commodities, even though ethicists have worked hard to protect them from becoming mere property that someone owns and can therefore trade.

Two big changes have taken place in recent years. One is the rise of an illegal international trade in organs and, alongside it, a slow change in attitudes toward payment. The second shift brings us directly to biotech and the new ethics agenda, for it involves the unambiguous sale and purchase of the most precious of all parts of the human body, sperm and eggs—the "gametes"—the reproductive cells that enable us to have children and that carry our genetic fingerprint. As we shall see in depressing detail in chapter 7, human eggs and semen are traded freely on the Internet. Some other countries regulate or ban such activities, but in the US there is a free-for-all.

The shift toward a trade in organs and the rapid development of a marketplace for eggs and sperm offer grim examples of the way our culture is moving. And they show how easy it is for us to smudge the distinction between people and property as the new biotech issues come on stream.

Commodities are, by definition, "raw materials" – things out of which we generally make something else. Even tea and coffee go through processes that turn a leaf or a bean into the dry powder that in due course gets infused with hot water to give us a beverage. That takes our use of the "commodification" image to another level. And it is in this sense that human nature is in the process of being turned, definitively, into a commodity.

Alongside the treatment of our body parts as "things" like tea and tin, our bodies as a whole are coming to be seen as merely complex machines. That theme runs through all of these new technologies. We are turning ourselves, creatures made by God, into creatures that *we* have made. When we use the word *creature*, we see afresh what we are doing. A creature is created, made by someone else. It is not just that we are treating ourselves like things; by seeking to take control not only of reproduction (that's what cloning does) but the design process itself (through genetics and other technologies), we become our own creators.

The builders of the Tower of Babel moved in exactly that arrogant direction. They wanted to make a name for themselves. By modern standards, their technology seems as pathetic as their aim. We know better. We have conquered the atom on the macroscale – think of the cyclotron that speeds up atomic particles at the Fermi Lab near Chicago, a piece of technology 1.3 miles across. We have mapped the human genome. We are devoting billions of dollars to nanotechnology to enable us to manipulate matter atom by atom. And we are building, not with slabs of sun-dried mud brick or quarried stone, but with the infinitely complex, microscopic, living stones that we have quarried from the human genome. We aim, not merely to build a tower that reaches to heaven, but a body confined to the earth. Unlike the

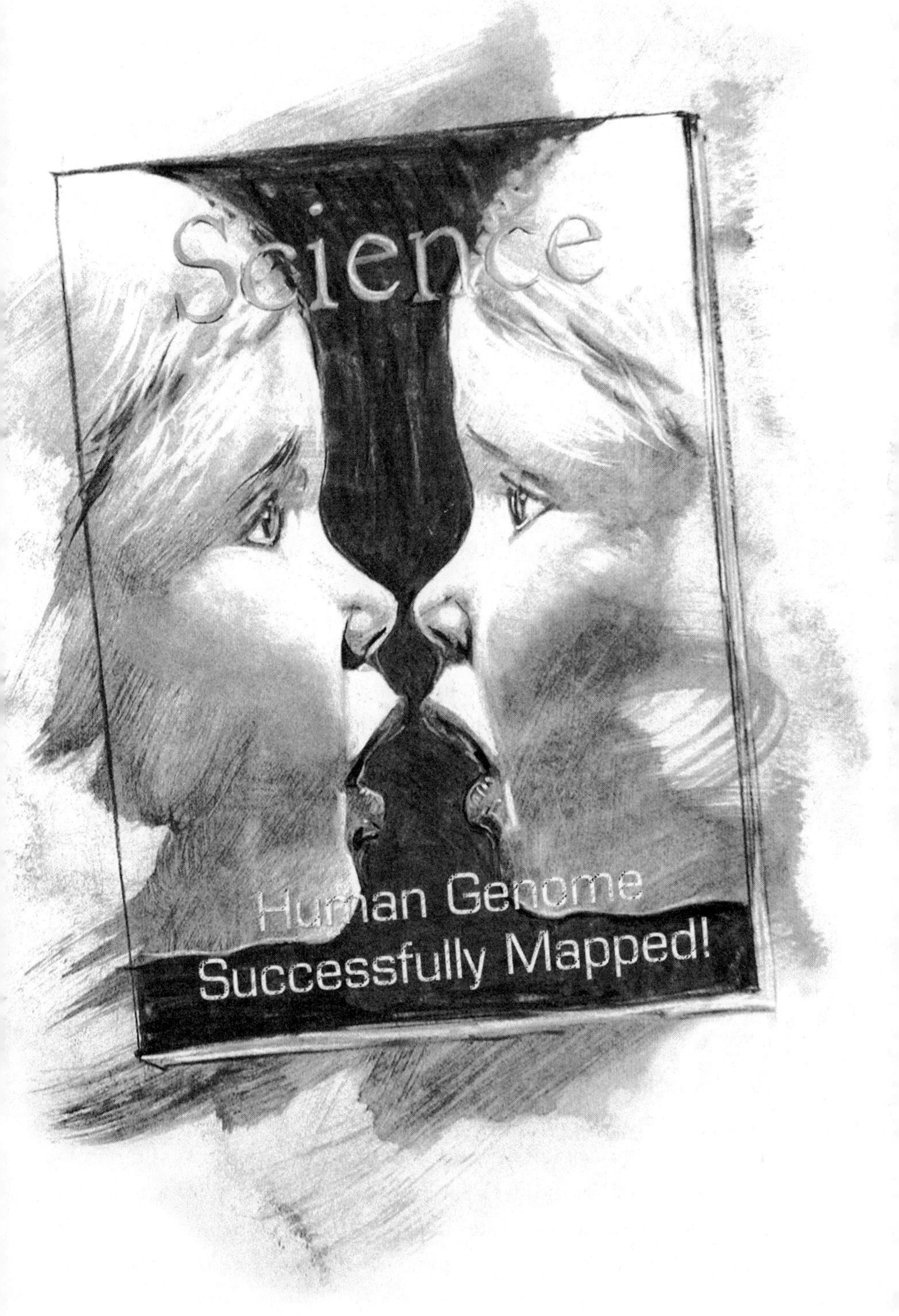
Science
Human Genome
Successfully Mapped!

builders of the tower, we don't just want to make a name for ourselves. We want to make *ourselves*. What the builders of Babel began, we may soon be in a position to finish.

ABORTION AND AMERICAN CULTURE

It will be many years before we finally understand the impact that abortion has had on our culture: millions of babies aborted, a generation mutilated by the wanton death of its children and siblings. Already some of its economic effects have been calculated—cutting the birthrate and making Western nations increasingly dependent on immigration at a time when, it is now widely agreed, the "population bomb" was a hoax.

Yet when the history books finally get written, two huge impacts of abortion will emerge that today go largely unnoticed. And, taken together, they go to the heart of the problem addressed in this book.

THE FREE-FIRE ZONE

First, abortion has placed the unborn child in a free-fire zone. Whatever the motives of those who favor it and have argued in defense of "abortion rights," *Roe v. Wade* has drawn a veil over the human dignity of unborn human life. It has opened the way to something very different from abortion, yet which has the same effect as killing the developing child: the use of human embryos in experiments and as sources for experimental material such as stem cells. Pro-choice campaigners never had this in mind. Some of them are happy about it; others (as we will see later) are not.

Thirty years of liberal abortion in America has declared life before birth off-limits to the protections of human dignity. Even pro-choice bioethics experts, who in the past opposed embryo experiments, have shifted their ground in the face of the fashionable attractions of embryonic stem cell research. The fact that an unborn child's life may be ended by his or her mother's choice, whatever her reasoning and situation—thus rendering the states powerless to intervene—has profoundly shaped the way in which we perceive the unborn. The momentum to declare early embryos suitable for experiments has proved nearly unstoppable.

The best example of this corruption of the American imagination became evident when "pro-life" Senator Orrin Hatch (Republican of Utah) decided, first, that because "life begins in the womb not the refrigerator," "spare" in vitro embryos may be used for experiments; and, second, that cloned embryos are not the same thing as embryos that resulted from fertilization and can therefore be manufactured for the purpose.

Roe has declared unborn human life a free-fire zone.

Pro-life Versus Pro-choice?

Second, abortion has radically divided "pro-life" and "pro-choice" advocates. Of course, these groups have wrestled mightily since *Roe* and made "the right to life" and "abortion rights" the most potent slogans in American culture. Abortion also has largely powered the entry of evangelicals and fundamentalists into public life, including such organizations as the Moral Majority and the Christian Coalition. An earlier generation of evangelical leaders had taken a softer view of abortion and treated it as a generally "Catholic" issue, like contraception. The move into firmer opposition against abortion proved an engine of evangelical–Catholic cooperation. On the political front, abortion has emerged for many Christians as *the* defining issue of their political engagement.

By the same token, support for "abortion rights" has proved a powerful organizing idea among progressive feminists, for whom "reproductive rights" have taken center stage in their understanding of the rights and dignity of women. Central to those rights has been abortion on demand. Any perceived limitation – through such initiatives as parental notification in the case of minors – has been strongly opposed.

Of course, we have both pro-life political progressives and pro-choice political conservatives. In general, the pro-life position has been on the defensive among Democrats, with leaders such as Al Gore moving from pro-life to pro-choice positions. At the same time, the libertarianism that affects both sides of the spectrum has made persistent gains on the right. Of course, not all evangelicals are politically conservative, and African American evangelicals tend to vote Democratic.

The point is this: the sudden emergence of the biotech agenda with the cloning controversy has shed fresh light on these broad social divisions, because pro-life and pro-choice have discovered they have something in common. Richard Doerflinger, who represents the Catholic bishops in these debates, gave testimony in favor of a ban on cloning at a House of Representatives committee hearing. Next to him, making the same case, sat Judy Norsigian, editor of the famous pro-choice feminist book *Our Bodies, Ourselves.* And further down the line sat Professor Stuart Newman, a founding member of the Council for Responsible Genetics, an explicitly pro-choice group of scientists who have been critical of many aspects of biotech and who oppose all experimental use of human embryos.

When Congresswoman Diane DeGette quizzed Judy Norsigian on how she could oppose cloning for research, Judy gave a dramatic reply: "The embryo isn't nothing." Moreover, pro-choice feminists have expressed anxiety about other aspects of the movement to clone embryos for experiments, including the risk to women's health in collecting the human eggs needed to produce human clones and the economic exploitation of poorer women that results from the offering of financial inducements to egg "donors."

Listen to these words:

> These technologies are being developed at a frenzied pace. The general public has had little real opportunity to understand and consider their full implications. There are few significant controls over their use.
>
> These conditions leave us vulnerable to being pushed into a new era of eugenic engineering, one in which people quite literally become manufactured artifacts. The implications for individual integrity and autonomy, for family and community life, for social and economic justice and indeed for world peace are chilling. Once humans begin cloning and genetically engineering their children for desired traits we will have crossed a threshold of no return.

We could have written such words. C. S. Lewis could have written them. Any thinking, serious Christian could endorse their message and grasp their profound significance. Yet they form the key section of a letter signed by Judy Norsigian and a hundred leaders of the pro-choice, "progressive" community! Some of them want a complete cloning ban. They compromised with a demand in the letter for a complete ban on cloning for "reproductive" purposes and a five-year ban on so-called "therapeutic" cloning.

Some in the "progressive" community have opposed any research on the embryo—not because they consider the embryo to be made in the divine image or to have the right to life, but because they see the embryo as deserving some degree of special respect. They feel alarmed that embryo research will lead to the redesign of human nature itself, through changes in the "germline" (the cells that carry our genetic inheritance). And they wish to protect women from having their eggs "harvested" for research.

Do we view this glass as at least half full? The conscience of the left has preserved much of the concern for the dignity of the individual (and our stewardship of creation) that less conscientious elements on the political right have let slip. This helps to provoke us into a deep discussion of the meaning of technology and a haunting review of the sad story of eugenics. For this we must thank our feminist and environmentalist friends.

Key supporters of "abortion rights" have included mainline Christian denominations, to the great sadness of many of their members. One of the major players has been the United Methodist Church, which maintains an explicit pro-choice view. Yet here also we see a clear distinction being drawn between support for the pro-choice abortion position and opposition to experiments involving cloned embryos.

We may think them inconsistent in their view of technology and the embryo. But each of these groups—pro-choice feminists, environmentally conscious scientists, and this mainline-liberal denomination—has an interest in the wider implications of biotechnology. Pro-life Christians may find this ironic, but alongside support for abortion, political progressives have long been critical of the development of biotech. The cloning issue has had the practical effect of drawing these warring parties into a loose coalition.

A powerful symbol of these developments appeared prominently in the op-ed pages of the *Chicago Tribune* on August 8, 2001. Two people well-known in their communities as symbols of the pro-choice and pro-life causes, respectively – law professor and widely published biotech writer Lori B. Andrews and Nigel M. de S. Cameron – coauthored the piece. It argued that the House of Representatives cloning hearing that brought together Judy Norsigian, Stuart Newman, and conservatives like Richard Doerflinger to argue on the same side of the cloning argument represented a watershed moment in the history of our time. It indicated that, while the abortion debate continued and would continue to be pursued with passion by both sides, farsighted leaders had chosen to come together and make common cause against a new threat to human dignity on which they were united.

Both the left and right are discovering, much to their surprise, that they agree on some major issues. In a classic illustration of what Francis Schaeffer termed "co-belligerency," they have discovered a common enemy.

There is little doubt that the biotech industry and its cheerleaders in the press and politics want the abortion debate to divide conservatives and progressives, making them unable to collaborate on anything else. The press has generally presented the debate as another round of *Roe*, with pro-lifers once again going into battle to defend the unborn. Press reporting of the House hearing with Norsigian, Newman, and Doerflinger is a case in point; it should have made headline news. It didn't.

As the "biotech century" opens, and the prospect of the brave new world dawns, Christians find themselves working with strange bedfellows. But we have been here before. William Wilberforce, the nineteenth-century British statesman, devoted his life to getting slavery abolished in the British empire through exactly such a strategy. More recently, it is how Christians have worked in Washington, DC, to expose the horrors of the concentration camps of North Korea and to press for an end to slavery and genocide in the Sudan. We always welcome the opportunity to work with men and women in the cause of what is just and right, even if we also disagree very deeply with other things they believe. As we examine the challenges of the brave new world in the chapters that follow, we will see that at many points we have allies in the struggle for human dignity. We thank God for them.

More than ever, the world needs prudence. The dictionary defines prudence this way: "to exercise sound judgment in practical matters, to be cautious or discreet in conduct, to be circumspect and not rash."

Just consider a recent incident involving Dr. Paul Agutter, a scientist jailed for seven years after trying to poison his wife. Dubbed "the Safeway Poisoner" because he tried to cover his tracks by spiking drinks with poison in a Safeway supermarket, Dr. Agutter has been released from a British prison and employed by the University of Manchester. Strangely, he's been hired to lecture students on ethics, including teaching a one-day course called "Therapeutic Cloning: Ethics and Science."

I would say the review committee at the University of Manchester lacked prudence on this one. Haven't its members looked at their moral compass lately? Don't they see something odd about their decision? When questioned, Dr. Piers Benn of Imperial College London defended the decision: "Normally, people who get into moral philosophy do so because they care about making the world a better place or putting things right. But I can't see any logical contradiction between being able to think about ethical questions and being able to do rather criminal acts."

What is a "rather" criminal act? Would Mrs. Agutter or the people who became sick after buying drinks at Safeway say they were "rather poisoned"?

Don't think cases like this are occurring mainly in the United Kingdom. They crop up in the States all the time. Princeton University, for example, employs Dr. Peter Singer, an ethics professor who advocates the killing of some unwanted persons. Infants born with severe disabilities are "pre-persons," in his judgment, and grandmothers with Alzheimer's are "post-persons." Dr. Singer believes that personhood is defined by an individual's ability to make decisions, to be "self-aware" or have self-consciousness. If a person lacks those mental faculties—or if he has extreme physical abnormalities—that individual should not be classed as a person. And, of course, if a human being is not considered a person, he has no rights. Dr. Singer's moral compass needs serious adjustment.

That adjustment, of course, can come only from the transcendent and eternal Word of God. Second Kings 18:32 insists, "Choose life and not death!" And Deuteronomy 30:19 - 20 says, "Now choose life, so that you and your children may live and that you may love the LORD your God, listen to his voice, and hold fast to him. For the LORD is your life." Acts 17:28 tells us that "in [God] we live and move and have our being." Without accepting strong and robust absolute truths like these, the pointer on our compass spins out of control, wildly swinging this way and that. God and his Word make up true north. The Prince of Peace is our Polaris. Without a grounding in God, anything — absolutely anything — goes.

I don't believe most people want to live in an out-of-control culture. I'm convinced people of common sense yearn for a society lawfully ordered. Despite what happened last week …

I received a letter from a man I will call Conrad who took issue with my views on Dr. Agutter. Conrad believed I was being uncharitable. He thought that if the doctor had paid his debt to society, he should be given every opportunity to get integrated back into the mainstream of life. This man chided me for my un-Christian spirit and lack of forgiveness. The letter stung. I wondered about the prudent thing to do. Rather than allow a reviling spirit to shape my response, I went to prayer. I asked God to: "Search me, O God, and know my heart; test me and know my anxious thoughts. See if there is any offensive way in me, and lead me in the way everlasting" (Psalm 139:23 - 24).

An hour later, I typed my reply:

Dear Conrad,

I want you to know your letter arrived safely. Thanks so much for taking time to express your concerns regarding my views on Dr. Agutter's position at the university.

On one hand, Conrad, I'm in agreement that when a convicted felon serves his sentence, he should be given every opportunity to be fully integrated back into society — it reflects the heart of Christ. I'm also grateful that, no doubt, opportunities for him in the scientific community

abound, and I wish him every success in his reinstatement in the field
of practical science.

But Dr. Agutter has been hired to teach ethics. And as a teacher,
he will oversee young students who look not only to his qualifications,
but to the practice of ethics in his life's experience. A teacher of ethics
brings character, discernment, wisdom, and insight into his field, guiding
students by experience and expertise.

Yes, Dr. Agutter's payment of penalty to society is complete. His
forgiveness—should he seek it from those he harmed—ought to be
assured. However, in my opinion his credibility and authority as a
teacher of ethics has been forfeited. Yes, his credibility and authority in
a scientific lab may be absolutely unquestioned; but not so his integrity
in standards of conduct and moral judgment which make for the basis
of good ethics. That will take time, much time, to reinstate.

Again, thank you for writing and I hope I've been able to explain
why I'm so concerned about not only this issue, but many other matters
which require good men of great character to lead and guide us with
integrity and sound judgment. It's what our society—it's what our
world—desperately needs.

Yours in His care,
Joni Eareckson Tada

George Will once stated that culture is like a giant slab of molasses
and our decisions, like tiny channels, guide its lumbering movement. And
so with much prayer and maybe more prudence, write that letter. Engage
your professor. Share your views with your neighbor, at the cleaners,
the community center, the market, or your neighborhood meeting place.
Influence culture and paint black "black" and white "white." Write your
local newspaper ... connect with your senator or city councillor.

In short, pull out your compass—your Bible—and point your world
due north.

JONI

CHAPTER 3

WONDERFULLY MADE

The other night I lay in bed watching the PBS channel. An award-winning show called *Life's Greatest Miracle* came on, offering an inside look into the hidden world of the conception of a baby and its development inside the womb. Swedish photographer Lennart Nilsson amazed me with his camera work as his tiny lens followed a million sperm into the wide, dark cavity of a woman's body.

The tiny sperm, their tails wriggling and heads bobbing, found themselves in thick gelatin, at which point the narrator intoned, "They are immediately in peril. The vagina is acidic; so they must escape, or die. Even in a healthy man, 60 percent of the sperm are less than perfect — like this one with two tails. For these guys, the journey is over. But what about the rest? What are the chances that one tiny sperm will reach and fertilize the egg? Sperm are often portrayed as brave little warriors fighting their way through a hostile environment in order to conquer the egg. Nothing could be further from the truth."

Next, I learned the egg definitely has a say in how things proceed. Apparently for most of the month, the cervix is shut tightly and clogged with a thick layer of mucous to keep out bacteria. But for a short time, for a few days a month around ovulation, the mucous becomes watery and forms tiny channels in which the sperm can swim through the cervix. My mouth dropped in wonder.

Once inside the uterus, the sperm still remain six inches from their goal, the egg. It'll be a two-day swim for them through all sorts of obstacles. The camera followed them as far as the opening to the fallopian tube. The sperm huddled at the base of the huge, hollow, forbidding cylinder. "How are they going to get up *that*?" I wondered aloud. The next image showed strings of mucous — a response of the fallopian tube to the change in uterine chemistry — resulting in little "highways" on which the sperm could continue their trek.

Halfway up the fallopian tube, more obstacles waited. I stared breath-less, gripped by one thought: *There's no way the sperm and egg are ever going to meet. No way will a baby come out of this alive.* Even when the egg and sperm finally met — no easy feat — there was a long way to go before the fertilized egg could survive the 50 percent rate of failure. In one quick action, the egg sent out a chemical to harden its shell, permitting no other sperm to pass through. Next, it began the long process of expel-ling half its chromosomes into a small pouch. After that, many steps had to take place before the tiny zygote — a one-celled embryo — would begin dividing.

By the time the embryo reached a recognizable stage, I had given up. I had surrendered. I simply could not comprehend it all, let alone process it. I kept repeating Psalm 139:14, "I praise you because I am fearfully and wonderfully made; your works are wonderful, I know that full well." The awesome timing of each stage of development, and how one process perfectly influenced another with all its enzymes and proteins, was, well … just as the PBS special was titled. It *was* the greatest miracle.

David the psalmist never had the benefit of intrauterine photography or a degree in biochemistry, but no one could say it better than he did in Psalm 139:15 - 17: "My frame was not hidden from you when I was made in the secret place. When I was woven together in the depths of the earth, your eyes saw my unformed body. All the days ordained for me were written in your book before one of them came to be. How precious to me are your thoughts, O God! How vast is the sum of them!"

By the way, the sperm and egg *did* make it. And so did the baby. When the camera focused on the pregnant mother in the delivery room, I almost gasped along with her. I realized I was about to wit-ness a real birth. First, you could see a tiny patch of hair, and then the rounded top of the baby's head; after more groans and pushing from the mother, there appeared the face, all red and smeared with blood and mucous. A doctor's hands gently turned the baby's head until one shoulder popped out, then the other. The next instant, the baby's body slipped out in a gush of fluid and flesh. Suddenly I found myself crying and laughing at the same time, stunned that such a tiny infant had not only survived, but survived whole and healthy, from head to toe. I kept shaking my head and enjoying the rush from the miraculous journey

I had just witnessed—a nine-month journey crammed into a one-hour PBS special.

Thousands, maybe millions of things could have gone wrong in that nine months, but everything—absolutely everything—went right. And not just for this one child, but for most of the 266 babies born into the world each minute.

We *are* fearfully and wonderfully made.

JONI

As the twentieth century morphs into the twenty-first and technology explodes around us, the Bible becomes more relevant every day. Especially the beginning of the Bible.

Christians believe that God gave us the Bible for all times, to teach us what to believe and how to live. He knew the challenges and problems we would face—not just as individuals but as nations and cultures and as one human race. He laid down principles that would enable us to understand and to do right.

That does not mean that we can expect to look up *cloning* or *genetics* in a concordance and find a Bible text that talks about these new ideas. Some people conclude that therefore God does not care what we do about these new technologies. They remind us of the woman who didn't want to see a psychiatrist because no psychiatrists appear in the Bible. "What about dentists?" answered her friend. "Don't you go to see them, either?"

In fact, the continuing relevance of the Bible *depends* on its not going into endless detail and giving all the particulars. If it did that for people in Old Testament times, how could it still speak to us in the twenty-first century?

The Bible therefore emphasizes *the foundation stones of truth*, the basic ideas that set the framework for our understanding of human life and its challenges. It sets out broad principles. And nowhere does it do so more effectively or relevantly than when it comes to biotech. If you want to understand how God looks at biotech, get into the beginning of the book of Genesis—and stay there.

The reason is actually very simple. What is biotech all about? In this book, we are looking at it, chapter by chapter, piece by piece—its threats, its promise. It can seem complicated. But back of all that, it remains remarkably simple. Biotech is about what it means to be human, to be "one of us." It's about techniques that enable us to "do" things to ourselves and to others, good and bad; and every one of them assumes a certain view of what it *means* to be one of us, or it assumes that it does not matter (in other words, that we don't know or care who we are). Christians know what others in our culture have forgotten: the secret of who we are. That's why we are uniquely placed to help our society decide how to handle biotech and its challenges. It's also why

Christians should not find it difficult to get their bearings on the moral issues in this debate.

If the biotech agenda is all about what it means to be human, so is Genesis, and the beginning of Genesis especially. In Genesis we find the keys to our understanding of what it means to be human, to be made by God, to be serving him in his world. And side-by-side with learning what it means to be human, we learn what humans were made to do. These are enormous questions, but in principle they are also simple – and that is how they are laid out for us in the Bible. We need to grasp the simplicity of their truth, then work out in detail how to apply them to the amazingly complex and fast-changing questions that confront us at the start of the twenty-first century.

WHAT DOES IT MEAN TO BE HUMAN?

At the heart of every culture lies its idea of what it means to be "one of us." That is nowhere truer than in our culture, which for many hundreds of years has been governed by the assumptions of the Christian worldview. For all its many failings, Western culture owes a huge debt to the key Christian idea of the unique dignity of the individual. That idea, of course, did not fall from space. It drew on the best thinking of the ancient civilizations of Greece and Rome. But its origins lie in Genesis chapter 1 and its baseline that God made man, male and female, in his image.

Were that statement not in the Bible, it would be blasphemous! We get used to the words, but they have cataclysmic implications. Elsewhere in Genesis 1 we read of God making the various "kinds" of animals and birds and sea creatures. They reproduce "after their kind." The implication is that humankind is made "after God's kind." We are made within the confines of space and time to *image* – to mirror, to model – *the nature of God.*

That decides our view of human nature. All human beings are created equal, and equally precious, in the sight of God. Moreover, if we ask the question, central to so many bioethics issues – "When does life begin?" or "Is this really human life?" – we have a crystal-clear answer. What human life bears the image of God? *All* human life.

Every member of our species, *Homo sapiens*, are image bearers of God and thus reflect the dignity of God. That is the basic reason Christians believe all human life to be "sacred" – a word that means inviolable, to be protected, and a word that reminds us that the root of this "sacredness" lies in God. And that is true of every human being – however young or old, sick or healthy, deformed, handicapped, or limited in whatever way.

Human dignity, and the fact that all members of our species share in that dignity, is our starting point for the Christian understanding of what it means to be human. Much of the debate about medicine and bioethics in the past generation has focused on this single question. It lies behind every discussion of abortion and euthanasia and it sheds a startling light on so many of the biotech debates that have focused on whether very early human life is "human" at all, even though from fertilization (or cloning) the early embryo is undeniably 100 percent a member of *Homo sapiens*. It would, of course, be very convenient if the earliest and tiniest humans could be said *not* to be human. But it's a fraud, and the biology textbooks are clear: fertilization marks the beginning of the life of a new individual member of any mammal species, and that includes us.

Since corporations and scientists have a growing interest in making embryos for experiments and medical treatments, it is vital to be clear at this point. And the Bible supports the commonsense view that for some members of our species to be special, all must be special. If we find it hard to imagine that a tiny embryo bears God's image, we need to do two things.

First, we should remind ourselves of what we know about genetics. Though the embryo may be very tiny, from fertilization it is a highly complex, self-organizing system.

Second, we need to remind ourselves of what we know about the incarnation. Jesus became human at the moment Mary's egg became miraculously fertilized. At one point in his life, Jesus was an embryo. So Christians can have no doubt that the tiniest human being is a person in God's image.

The fact that God took human form in Jesus sheds unique light on the significance of being human. Human nature is so uniquely special that it is the kind of being that God can take for himself. The incarnation is what theologians call a "mystery," but that does not mean we can make no sense of it. Rather, it means we cannot entirely grasp it, can understand it only in part. By becoming human after making human nature in his image, God has twice placed his stamp on human dignity. And having taken on human nature in first-century Palestine, he has not given it up. Many believers do not realize that after his resurrection and ascension, Jesus did not abandon his human form. In the words of the creed, he "sat down on the right hand of God"—he took once more his glorious place as the Son of God in heaven, yet he retained his human nature alongside the divine. It would be hard to imagine any more startling way of underscoring the dignity of human nature than the belief that the Jesus we meet in glory will still have the glorified body he had on earth—still have human nature alongside the nature of God.

What does it mean to be human? To be human is to be made in the image of God, to bear unique dignity. And every human being—every member of our species—possesses that dignity. That is the starting point.

WHY GOD PUT US HERE

Genesis 1 does not stop there. It goes on to set out the two basic purposes for which God put his human creatures on the earth: the task of procreation ("fill the earth") and the task of dominion ("and subdue it").

Of course, this "dominion" is not limited to the activities spelled out in Genesis 1 ("rule over the fish of the sea, over the birds of the air"). This is a perfect example of the key fact we already discussed: the Bible addresses the culture of its day, and at the same time lays down lasting principles for all cultures. The basic principle remains the same, whether applied to primitive ancient culture or the complex technological culture of today. Just as the list in Genesis 1 covers the various aspects of the life of an agricultural society, so we need to survey the parallel aspects of our very different experience. We are called to have dominion over government, the arts, the media, the life of the corporate world, the university—and science and technology.

Made in His Image — To Have Dominion

Then God said, "Let us make man in our image, in our likeness, and let them rule over the fish of the sea and the birds of the air, over the livestock, over all the earth, and over all the creatures that move along the ground." So God created man in his own image, in the image of God he created him; male and female he created them. God blessed them and said to them, "Be fruitful and increase in number; fill the earth and subdue it. Rule over the fish of the sea and the birds of the air and over every living creature that moves on the ground."

Genesis 1:26–28

Neither does the "procreation" task refer merely to the begetting and conception of children, but rather to their nurture in families and giving in marriage so that the human race continues and the earth is filled. Plainly, not all people have children; some are infertile, others remain single and childless. But the task given to humankind as a whole is clear. It is especially important to note that this task is set out quite separately from the "dominion" task. On the one hand, we are to procreate and fill the earth; on the other, we are to have dominion.

One reason why biotechnology is so challenging lies in the fact that it involves them both; in the words of Genesis 1, the filling of the earth and dominion over it. They come together, since technology — our means of making things — is used to help or replace sexual procreation. Here we find one cause of those problems: the turning of human procreation into a project in the exercise of our "dominion" over the earth.

So What Is Technology?

Technology does not need to be "high-tech." A spade or a hammer is still technology, just like a computer or the space shuttle. Technology is what humans use to carry out their "dominion" task — everything from tools they place in their hands to make their arms longer and their muscles more effective, to the complex machines produced by the ingenuity of thousands of thinkers and craftsmen over many generations.

Technology is technology. Yet technology is *not* simply neutral.

Most technologies can be used for good and evil purposes, though they may have a tendency in one direction rather than the other. A hammer can be used to knock nails into boards to make a house or to smash someone's head on a dark night. A computer can help run a church, a business, a terrorist cell, or a police state.

Take the example of pre-implantation genetic diagnosis, which we address further in a later chapter. This procedure uses genetics to screen embryos used during in vitro fertilization before they are implanted, the purpose of which is to decide if they should live or die. In vitro fertilization, as we have seen, springs the embryo and the process of fertilization from both the protection and the unknowns of the womb, and gives knowledge and options and opportunities that can lead to unethical actions.

Technologies can take on a sinister character with values of their own. Genetic information may have legitimate purposes (for example, enabling someone to have timely treatment for a genetic disorder or enabling a couple who may be carrying defective genes to be counseled about whether they should have children). Yet genetic information threatens to overwhelm the dignity and the freedom of the individual either because it is known to others (such as insurers, employers, and government), or simply to themselves and the families (giving years of anxiety before a late-onset condition, for example). At the private level, "good" genetic information can be as damaging as "bad." The 1997 movie *Gattaca* is so good because it shows this well. Two of the film's characters suffer because of their *good* genes: Jerome had managed to win only an Olympic silver medal, when his genes predicted a gold; and Anton, for all his expensive, genetically planned birth, ended up a "mere" policeman.

Technology, to be good, must serve the "dominion" command by enabling men and women to "subdue" the earth, and yet to do so in a manner that underscores the dignity of humankind and a stewardship-oriented view of the rest of nature.

THE BABEL PRINCIPLE

The first eleven chapters of Genesis include many extraordinary stories, but they all form part of one story: how God made the earth and set human beings and other creatures on it, and how God's human creatures disobeyed him. Through a series of narratives—all the way from the "fall" when Adam and Eve first disobey, to the call of Abraham that begins the story of Israel and the main narrative of the Old Testament—sin and judgment and grace get woven together to set the stage for the later story of humankind.

In the story of the ancient world, from the entry of sin at the fall until the flood brings it to an end and a new beginning, we read of two key events. They set out the two basic aspects to sin and its possibilities.

First, Cain commits the first great crime in history by murdering his brother, Abel. In this violent act, the children of Adam and Eve fall victim to the vicious power of sin. Their parents had been expelled from the paradise of Eden; and, soon after, we find one son dead and the other a killer. This precious thing, human life—life made in the image of God—is subject to the whim of humankind. In this first case of sibling rivalry, murder sets the stage for the compounding of sin as one chapter follows the last. This sorry history culminates in the great flood, where God's judgment on human violence leads to the near extinction of the human race and a gracious, fresh start that echoes the creation story itself.

Yet in the middle of the "covenant" with Noah—the first explicit covenant setting out the relationship between God and humankind—we find the first announcement of the penalty for the sin of murder. And it links us back to Genesis 1 and the kind of being that God had made his human creature to be. "Whoever sheds the blood of man, by man shall his blood be shed; for in the image of God has God made man" (Genesis 9:6).

The first great sin of homicide gets handled with grace. Cain receives a special "mark" intended to protect him even as he lives under the judgment of God. Ultimately the violence grows and spreads until it brings on the vast judgment of the flood that almost ends the life of the world. God regrets making humankind, but in grace he gives

The First Murder

Now Cain said to his brother Abel, "Let's go out to the field." And while they were in the field, Cain attacked his brother Abel and killed him. Then the LORD said to Cain, "Where is your brother Abel?" "I don't know," he replied. "Am I my brother's keeper?" The LORD said, "What have you done? Listen! Your brother's blood cries out to me from the ground."

GENESIS 4:8 – 10

the people made in his image a new beginning. They get a fresh start full of love, complete with a promise from God that he will never again send another worldwide flood. "As long as the earth endures, seedtime and harvest, cold and heat, summer and winter, day and night will never cease" (Genesis 8:22). Yet even at this new beginning we see that sin has not been washed away (think of the perverse story of Noah's drunkenness) – and we hear the somber institution of the death penalty for the crime of murder.

This takes us straight into the questions raised by bioethics. Early in the debate, the key issues focus on the sanctity of life, which have been challenged in abortion and euthanasia, as well as in subtler issues, such as organ transplants and the definition of death. The taking of human life, whether by homicide or by defining "human life" so as to exclude certain human beings (like the unborn and the elderly) from the dignity shared by the rest of the human race, is nothing but the sin of Cain.

Second, the story of the Tower of Babel in Genesis 11 describes the first great social act of human sin after the fall recounted in Genesis 3. Almost every children's Sunday school in the nation has a poster of the Tower of Babel somewhere on its classroom walls. We can easily imagine ourselves into the life of those men and women who devoted all their mental, financial, and physical energies to the construction of this greatest of ancient buildings. We feel struck with horror as we read that they intended it as a monument to themselves – so they could "make a name" for themselves apart from God. And we feel perplexed as well as awed by the judgment that it brought on them:

the "confusion of tongues" that dispersed the early human race and destroyed the capacity to freely collaborate, leaving men and women humbled and divided.

In striking contrast to Cain and Abel and the moral causes of the flood, this story focuses not on violence but on something very different. Indeed, by contrast with this story, Cain's homicide seems tawdry and crass. This is sin of another order. We see no violence here, no sexual immorality, no worship of "false gods"—nothing gross. We simply witness a building project—one of two great technology projects of the ancient world described for us in the book of Genesis. It may perplex us that it could have the significance given to it in Genesis. It actually helps that it does perplex us, because then we are prepared for our problem in assessing the technologies of our own day, as well as their often hidden significance: hidden from those who develop them;

The Tower of Babel

Now the whole world had one language and a common speech. As men moved eastward, they found a plain in Shinar and settled there.

They said to each other, "Come, let's make bricks and bake them thoroughly." They used brick instead of stone, and tar for mortar. Then they said, "Come, let us build ourselves a city, with a tower that reaches to the heavens, so that we may make a name for ourselves and not be scattered over the face of the whole earth."

But the Lord came down to see the city and the tower that the men were building. The Lord said, "If as one people speaking the same language they have begun to do this, then nothing they plan to do will be impossible for them. Come, let us go down and confuse their language so they will not understand each other."

So the Lord scattered them from there over all the earth, and they stopped building the city. That is why it was called Babel—because there the Lord confused the language of the whole world. From there the Lord scattered them over the face of the whole earth.

GENESIS 11:1–9

hidden also from believers as they observe and seek to make sense of what is happening. But not hidden from God!

Is Genesis telling us that technology *as such* is bad? Is it wrong to seek to extend our powers by either simple or complex means? Does such a pursuit insult God and deny our dependence on him? The Bible, as usual, provides its own answer.

We find not one great technology project in the book of Genesis, but two. Already we have discussed the significance of the flood as God's judgment on the spreading violence that began with the killing of Abel. This story dominates the early part of the book of Genesis, spanning three chapters and leading into the covenant with Noah. Yet from another perspective, the story of the flood is actually *the story of the ark*!

The ark is the first great technology project of the ancient world. The building of the ark, also prominently featured on Sunday school classroom walls, is described in far more detail than the building of the tower. Like the tower, we generally treat it as something for children! Yet as we seek to gain a biblical perspective on the explosive power of technology to change our culture and even ourselves, this is where we need to start.

One of the two great technology projects in Genesis symbolized humankind's rebellion against God and received his massive judgment. The other was a gift of God to humankind, to rescue the human race from the consequences of their own sin. Babel symbolized worldwide rebellion against God and humankind's sinful determination to use technology to go his own way; the ark represented God-honoring technology given to preserve the life that God had given. The contrast couldn't be stronger.

Technology *can* have a special value. The Babel principle represents rebellious technology, intended to enable humans to take over from God. It led to the scattering of the nations and the curse of enmity and division that has plagued the world ever since. Yet thousands of years later, in a form that could never before have been imagined, we see the Babel bug returning. Human technology has grown so potent that we think we have no need of God; it claims powers over our own species that will enable us to recreate ourselves in our own image.

That takes us back to Genesis 1 again, and also Genesis 3.

THE ROOT OF HUMAN SIN

At one level, the sin of Adam and Eve (that we call the "fall") occurred simply enough: Eve took and then they both ate a piece of fruit from a tree that God had explicitly told them not to eat. At another level, of course, what they did was as profound in its evil as it is hard to explain. Because in taking the fruit—in doing that one thing God had told them not to do—they declared their independence from God and placed both their own judgment and the authority of the Devil above him. This was no incidental act of disobedience; it was a declaration of war.

So it is no surprise that God responded in equal measure. He had issued a severe threat: "When you eat of it you will surely die." The punishment represented a more profound version of the threat: expulsion from the garden and the presence of God, ultimate mortality, and disorder of every kind, both within the creation and between the sub-human creation and humankind. All this and more gets spelled out in Genesis 3.

At heart, the fall challenged the authority of God and proudly declared human self-sufficiency. It rapidly led to family rivalry, the first homicide, and the wider violence that led to the judgment of the flood and God's institution of the death penalty as part of the new world order. Yet the blasphemy of killing someone made in God's image flows from the declaration of independence that came first.

The apostle Paul writes about Jesus in Philippians 2. In a famous hymn of praise that doubles as one of the deepest statements of theology in the Bible, the apostle speaks about Jesus' laying aside his privileges in heaven and voluntarily coming to earth, all the way to the cross, for us. In one telling phrase that directly compares him to Adam, Paul writes that Jesus "did not count equality with God something to be grasped." He makes two points at the same time.

First, Jesus was the genuine "equal" of God the Father, yet he chose to set aside that equality and voluntarily subject himself to taking human form, even to willingly accepting death on the cross. Not like Adam! That's the second point. Adam had *no* right to equality with God, and yet he "grasped" at it. Jesus laid aside what was his by right, in order to undo the fall precipitated by Adam's rebellion. In the chapters following Genesis 3, we follow the sad story of Adam's "grasping" at equality with God, leading to one terrible deed after another.

Yet grasping at equality with God is nowhere as clear as at Babel. For here the leaders of the world come together and make a common purpose: to make a name for themselves, to use their technology to "grasp equality with God." Their great monument does not bear the label *Soli Deo Gloria* (to the glory of God alone); it exalts themselves alone and bears only their own name.

President George W. Bush on Science and Ethics

Science has set before us decisions of immense consequence. We can pursue medical research with a clear sense of moral purpose or we can travel without an ethical compass into a world we could live to regret.

CLONING SPEECH, WHITE HOUSE, 2002

The Babel principle returns whenever humankind decides to exploit the God-given gifts of skill and strength and the plentiful resources of God's world to achieve power through technology. Every previous opportunity that humankind has faced to employ our skills to challenge the authority of God, from Babel on, has helped only to pave the way for the greatest challenge. That challenge comes not in the form of killing and destruction, from the crime of Cain to the wide-scale violence that brought the flood to the atrocities of Rwanda and Bosnia. Rather, it is the subtler and most sinister challenge of all: the threat, first, to turn the process of human procreation into a feat of manufacturing; and second (and worse yet), to seize the place of God the Creator in designing and redesigning human nature itself. That is the final embodiment of the sinful challenge to God: to use "our" technology to displace him; to make a name for ourselves in this, his world; to let loose the Babel principle in the technology of today, in which the principle remains unchanged and yet the propensity for evil grows infinitely greater.

The Ark or the Tower?

We need to honor God and each other–those are the clear lessons of the early chapters of the Bible. Whatever we do must remain focused both on him and on us. If once we separate ourselves from him–behave as if he were not there–using our skills and his gifts will destroy us. If, however, we use our talents to act as productive stewards in his world, with one eye on human dignity and the other on the God who stands behind it, we do well.

The question we face when we look at the biotech century ahead of us must always be: Is this the ark, God-given technology for our good? Or is it the tower, a symbol of our rebellion and something that will surely bring disaster on us?

"Why am I living? What's my purpose?" Not many have the guts to say it out loud, but lots of us think it. A slew of self-help books, midday talk shows, and one-hour counseling services offer to help us find meaning in life. Sometimes the purpose is hard to pin down in this quick-fix, fast-paced, no-deposit-no-return culture. Everything's so external. Disposable. Even people for whom there seems no "purpose" in living.

Consider Ryan, born with Crouzon's syndrome. The deformity eventually left him paralyzed, unable to speak, blind, and virtually deaf. He also needs a feeding tube in order to eat. That's a lot of baggage attached to a child! It's more baggage when you realize Ryan has outlived statistics and is now a young man in his twenties. If life's largest questions have answers for him, then there are answers for us all.

I met Ryan when his father, Doug Mazza, president of Joni and Friends, took me to his son's "graduation" from a special school. I watched Doug beam with pride as Ryan was wheeled into the gymnasium in a gown and cap. Afterward, Doug sat next to his son, kerker-derking his hat, talking and teasing, and giving Ryan good-natured hugs. This was one proud dad! Every once in a while Ryan lifted his head and smiled. At least, it seemed he was smiling.

"Is Ryan able to hear you?" I asked.

"For sure," Doug answered. "He knows it's me. When he whines, I'll press my cheek against him and talk in his ear. He knows it's me, don't cha, buddy?" he said, tousling his son's hair.

I leaned over to say hi to Ryan. I don't know if he heard me, but I would have sworn I saw a faint smile. He slumped slightly—a sign of fatigue, or of boredom with the cap-and-gown thing. I thought of the many experts who would say, "Take out his feeding tube. He can't do anything. His life has no meaning, no purpose." Privately they would surely add the costs involved in his housing, health care, schooling, and more.

I'm glad those people can't come after Ryan with their court orders and rogue judicial rulings. A lot of other disabled people aren't so fortunate. They don't have watchful fathers, like Ryan does. Some of them are not safe in their residential centers. Some have family members who abandon them to the system. No wonder impaired people feel threatened by "you're-better-off-dead-than-disabled" attitudes. Many in our culture have a fundamental fear—almost a terror—of accidents, injuries, old age, or birth defects. To them, the physical challenges seem so *futile.* So we run a cost-effective analysis on the strain a boy with Crouzon's syndrome places on the system to determine if he's worth the trouble and expense. If the love of money is the root of all kinds of evil—and it is—then a young man like Ryan is exposed and vulnerable.

That's *a lot* to counter. So I sat by Ryan and silently prayed that God would speak to him "in words taught by the Spirit, expressing spiritual truths in spiritual words" (1 Corinthians 2:13). I prayed that Ryan would be strengthened with "power through [God's] Spirit in [his] inner being" (Ephesians 3:16).

I considered again all the people who would label him a "nonperson." Who has the right to say such a thing? Where do we find the basis for ascribing value to life? What measuring rod do we use? Is there a supreme authority in this shifting world?

Jesus said in Matthew 16:26, "What good will it be for a man if he gains the whole world, yet forfeits his soul? Or what can a man give in exchange for his soul?" A soul is *at least* worth the wealth of the world. The buck stops—and starts—with the Bible. The Word of God is the sole voice that ascribes value to life – even life with Crouzon's syndrome. God breathed life into man and thereby permanently stamped his image – and his glory and greatness – on all who would ever draw breath.

This includes Ryan.

If 2 Corinthians 4:17 assures you and me that "our light and momentary troubles are achieving for us an eternal glory that far outweighs them all," then it's also valid for Ryan. If 2 Corinthians 4:16 reminds us that "inwardly we are being renewed day by day," then it's true for Ryan. If God "sustain[s] all things by his powerful word," then it includes Ryan (Hebrews 1:3). That young man with Crouzon's syndrome has his *being* – his essence and identity – in God. No wonder then "we fix our eyes not on what is seen, but on what is unseen" (2 Corinthians 4:18).

God's Spirit expresses truth to Doug's son, not in audible words, but spiritual words. Inwardly he is being renewed. His troubles are achieving for him an eternal glory. His value is "not on what is seen, but what is unseen." The Spirit is dynamic, kinetic, active, and powerful – and although we can't see the Spirit at work in Ryan's life, it's happening. We can't measure God's work, or quantify it, but it's real. And spiritual activity imparts value and purpose to that life, no matter how humble the circumstances. Therefore, we cannot regard Ryan – and people like him – from a worldly point of view.

This is what gives Ryan's life meaning.

When we stand before Jesus, Ryan may end up achieving greater accolades than any of us. Just think: he is perfectly demonstrating – even if by default – gentleness and self-control, the fruit of the Holy Spirit. His life illustrates patience, endurance, and consummate long-suffering. He does not complain or lash out. In fact, when he cries, whether due to pain or fear, Ryan immediately responds to the smallest of loving touches – the brush of a hand on his cheek.

In so doing, Ryan inspires everyone who takes time to sit next to him and feel his courage. And he's doing it all without lifting a finger, winking an eye, or speaking a word of encouragement. I felt it. I saw it. And I'm the richer for it.

True, he's not doing much more than being. But that's God's problem, "for in him we live and move and have our being" (Acts 17:28). Ryan is a perfect example of Acts 1:8, which says, "You will *be* my witnesses" (italics mine).

God has his reasons. He has his purposes. He never does things capriciously or decides with the flip of a coin. Ryan's God—the God of the Bible—our God, your God, is an intentional God, brimming over with motive and mission; and his design for that young man is to simply live, breathe, and encourage others. Others like you ...

It's enough to give life meaning and purpose.

JONI

CHAPTER 4

THE BETTER BABIES STORY

I was thirty-nine years old, lying on my gynecologist's table and watching my biological clock tick away. Dr. Fox, an infertility specialist, was trying his best to help my husband and me become pregnant. This would be Ken's and my third checkup to see if any of our quick-get-the-thermometer-stand-on-your-head gymnastics paid off with the longed-for words from my doctor, "Joni, you're pregnant!"

It wasn't to be.

On the way home from the doctor's office, I broke down. Never had such gut-wrenching, heart-twisting sobs flooded from my soul. I felt devastated. For a brief few hours, I panicked. *There must be a way. I have to become pregnant. Surely there must be an option, a new treatment, something Ken and I haven't tried!*

Now, years later, I realize I had been *consumed* by my passion to have a child. When a natural instinct becomes that strong and overwhelming, it has become an obsession. In today's cultural climate (a climate that can offer a childless couple an amazing smorgasbord of reproductive options), it can become an idol. The creative authority of God gets shoved aside, replaced by the idol of reproductive technology. Isaiah 2:8 – 9 describes our society well: "Their land is full of idols; they bow down to the work of their hands, to what their fingers have made. So man will be brought low and mankind humbled."

It's been almost two decades since my visit to Dr. Fox. The urgent desire for children has dissipated, supplanted by the many happy relationships Ken and I enjoy with boys and girls of all ages. I look at today's couples who restlessly explore the salad bar of technological advancements — each treatment and procedure more dangerous and daring than the last — and I realize it's no longer a matter of "We want a child"; it's "We want the *perfect* child."

We never feel satisfied when beguiled by idols. We become enslaved by the very thing we desperately seek and, in so doing, we lose our bearings. We lose what it truly means to "have a baby."

Our land is full of idols. We've become entranced by the technological work of our hands and convinced that with each advance, humankind is being exalted. Little do we realize ... we are about to be brought low. About to be humbled.

It may be the only way to save humankind.

JONI

Back in the middle of the nineteenth century, while Charles Darwin was writing about the "survival of the fittest" as the driving force behind his idea of evolution, his cousin, Francis Galton, came up with another idea: getting superior men and women to marry each other so that their children would be "fitter." Eugenics literally means "good genes," and at the beginning of the twentieth century this way of thinking used the new science of genetics to build a movement for the breeding of better people. It fast became one of the dominant movements in America in the first part of the century. This chapter tells a sad story we all need to remember one hundred years later.

The goal of eugenics is to have healthy, attractive, gifted babies in order to have better, more productive, and happier adults. Of course, some problems with this approach seem obvious. Healthy, attractive, gifted people are, in fact, no more likely to be happy than disabled, ugly, or dumb people. If happiness is the goal, this is not the best way to go. It's well known that the genetic abnormality known as Down syndrome produces people who are generally happier than the rest of us. It is also the case that cats are generally much more content than their owners, but we don't all want to be cats. The search for "happiness" has always eluded us. But eugenics was driven even more by the idea that *the rest of us* will be happier (and wealthier) without "inferior" people around.

When most people hear the word *eugenics* they think of the Germany of the 1930s and 1940s and the terrible crimes committed by the Nazis. But the Nazis did not invent eugenics; they simply built on ideas from America. In his powerful book *The War against the Weak*, Edwin

Black, a best-selling writer on the Holocaust, takes us back in depressing detail to the enormously popular eugenics industry that caught the diseased imagination of the United States in the first part of the last century. His subtitle says it all: *Eugenics and America's Campaign to Create a Master Race.*

Black explains how the eugenicists got organized with funding from the great philanthropists of the day (Rockefeller, Carnegie, and Harriman):

> In 1904, the Carnegie Institution established a laboratory complex at Cold Spring Harbor on Long Island that stockpiled millions of index cards on ordinary Americans, as researchers carefully plotted the removal of families, bloodlines and whole peoples. From Cold Spring Harbor, eugenics advocates agitated in the legislatures of America, as well as the nation's social service agencies and associations.

This project was known as the "Eugenics Record Office," which made it sound official—and it built card indexes based on the private information of millions of Americans, much of it obtained without the subjects' permission from hospitals and other public institutions. Here is an example of how it worked in the state of Virginia:

> A single day in the 1930s was typical. The Montgomery County sheriff drove up unannounced onto Brush Mountain and began one of his many raids against the hill families considered socially inadequate. More precisely, these hill families were deemed "unfit," that is, unfit to exist in nature. On this day the Montgomery County sheriff grabbed six brothers from one family, bundled them into several vehicles and then disappeared down the road. Earlier, the sheriff had come for the boys' sister. Another time, deputies snared two cousins....

These mountain people were systematically sterilized under a Virginia law compelling such operations for those ruled unfit.

Black's source for this particular story? A former Montgomery County supervisor, many years later. In his book, Black chronicles the history of the Eugenics Record Office and the other institutions of American eugenics. He demonstrates US leadership in the worldwide movement and the support of American statesmen for the project: it was the US Secretary of State who sent out the invitations to the first worldwide eugenics conferences. He sets out in damning detail the linkages between foundations such as the Rockefellers' and not only American eugenics but the eugenics research of the Nazis themselves. Just before the outbreak of war in 1939, Josef Mengele's university boss, to whom he later sent his samples and records from Auschwitz, was still supported by American foundation money.

Eugenics was an idea whose time seemed to have come in the early twentieth century. But since the Nazis adopted it and took it to its logical conclusion, it soon disappeared from respectable company. Black notes that "eugenics" quickly morphed into "genetics." Societies and journals changed their names to this more "scientific" term as eugenics became unpopular. Black warns of a "newgenics" to come, as the Carrie Buck mindset makes a comeback in the biotech age of far more sophisticated technology.

But who was Carrie Buck?

THE CARRIE BUCK STORY

One key to eugenics is to see it as a search for what might be considered "other people's happiness." The child with Down syndrome is rarely the center of discussion once the debate begins. Typically, concern surrounds the family members, caretakers, and others who are presumably burdened by the one who has yet to die or who was born with some type of physical deficiency. Disabled people who don't meet the current criteria of "attractiveness" embarrass other people. They cause inconvenience. There may be an associated financial burden. These are the motivations that lie behind the infamous decision of the US Supreme Court in *Buck v. Bell.*

Carrie Buck was born out of wedlock in 1906 to Emma Harlow, who was then married to Frank Buck. Carrie had two half-siblings born to two different fathers. At four years of age Carrie was given up for adoption. Until she reached the sixth grade, Carrie showed no signs of mental impairments. At puberty, according to record, Carrie began to cause trouble. When she was eighteen, she became pregnant and gave birth to a daughter, and Carrie's adoptive family requested that she be institutionalized. So, in January 1924, eighteen-year-old Carrie Buck was committed to a state institution because the Juvenile and Domestic Court of Charlottesville ruled her to be "epileptic and feeble-minded." At the institution, Carrie's primary physician, Dr. Albert S. Priddy, signed an order for her mandatory sterilization. Her appointed guardian took the case to court. Judge Bennett T. Gorgon of the Circuit Court of Amherst County ruled in April of 1925 that the sterilization of Carrie Buck was constitutional. The guardian appealed the ruling and the case then went to the Virginia Supreme Court of Appeals. The decision to move forward with the sterilization was upheld by the Virginia Supreme Court of Appeals, and the appeal continued all the way to the US Supreme Court.

The Supreme Court case of *Buck v. Bell* provides a telling display of the American eugenics movement at work. The defense argued that Carrie Buck should be involuntarily sterilized because it was better for society if her hereditary traits were not passed on to another generation. Descriptions of Carrie Buck included things such as having a life

of "immorality, prostitution, and untruthfulness." During the case lawyers argued that Carrie could not sustain herself, and since she already had an illegitimate child whom she could not care for, her ability to reproduce should be terminated.

Documentation concerning the life of Carrie's mother also made it into the case. Lawyers pointed out that Emma Harlow's life also had a record of immorality, prostitution, and untruthfulness. These traits were attributed to Carrie as "feeblemindedness." The Eugenics Record Office tried to offer a genetic account of her "feeblemindedness" as a trait passed down through her mother. At one point during the trial, an expert witness stated of Carrie Buck, her mother, and child that "these people belong to the shiftless, ignorant, and worthless class of anti-social whites of the South." On May 2, 1927, the Court approved the sterilization of Carrie Buck, upholding the Virginia stat-

ute and other state laws that deemed compulsory sterilization constitutional in people considered genetically unfit. Supreme Court Justice
Oliver Wendell Holmes Jr. – by far the most famous judge of his day –
delivered the opinion of the court: "It is better for all the world, if
instead of waiting to execute degenerate offspring for crime, or to let
them starve for their imbecility, society can prevent those who are
manifestly unfit from continuing their kind.... Three generations of
imbeciles are enough."

who are the fathers

The eugenicists could not have been more pleased with the out-
come. It not only demonstrated that their view agreed with the Constitution, it also greatly encouraged the use of existing sterilization
statutes and the passing of more.

The IQ tests used on Carrie Buck have long since been discredited.
Little evidence suggests that Carrie and her family came up seriously
short in intellect. It seems clear that Carrie and her mother got locked
away in institutions because they did not conform; people simply did
not approve of their behavior. Sadly, Carrie Buck's daughter, Vivian,
died of an intestinal disorder while in the second grade; her teachers
and others reported that she was very smart.

Meanwhile, eugenic sterilization laws spread to nearly thirty states,
California being among the most important. Black writes:

> In 1909, California became the third state to adopt such
> laws. Ultimately, eugenics practitioners coercively sterilized
> some 60,000 Americans, barred the marriage of thousands,
> forcibly segregated thousands in "colonies," and persecuted
> untold numbers in ways we are just learning. Before World
> War II, nearly half of coercive sterilizations were done in
> California, and even after the war, the state accounted for a
> third of all such surgeries.

California was considered an epicenter of the American eugenics
movement. During the twentieth century's first decades, California's
eugenicists included potent but little-known race scientists, such as US
Army venereal disease specialist Dr. Paul Popenoe, citrus magnate
Paul Gosney, Sacramento banker Charles Goethe, as well as members

of the California State Board of Charities and Corrections and the University of California Board of Regents.

Eugenics in America

But the leaders of the eugenics movement did not limit their activities to incarceration and sterilization. In 1920 they conducted the first of many "fitter family" contests at the Kansas Free Fair. "Fitter Families" were judged on their physical health, records of heredity, educational attainments, and measurable intellectual capacities. Winning families received a medal that carried the logo, "Yea, I Have a Goodly Heritage." The eugenics movement propagated the belief that environment played little part in determining character and achievement. Instead, leaders taught that bad character traits resulted from bad genes.

The tragic story of the wide embrace of eugenics in America is told vividly on the website *www.eugenicsarchive.org*. As Christine Rosen has shown in her fine book *Preaching Eugenics*, the churches – and synagogues – had a key role in promoting the eugenics agenda, which was driven by racism as well as the pseudo-science of eugenics itself. Edwin Black puts it like this:

> The superior species the eugenics movement sought was populated not merely by tall, strong, talented people. Eugenicists craved blond, blue-eyed Nordic types. This group alone, they believed, was fit to inherit the Earth. In the process, the movement intended to subtract emancipated Negroes, immigrant Asian laborers, Indians, Hispanics, East Europeans, Jews, dark-haired hill folk, poor people, the infirm and anyone classified outside the gentrified genetic lines drawn up by American raceologists.

> How? By identifying so-called defective family trees and subjecting them to lifelong segregation and sterilization programs to kill their bloodlines. The grand plan was literally to wipe away the reproductive capability of those deemed weak and inferior – the so-called unfit. The eugenicists hoped to neutralize the viability of 10 percent of the population at a sweep, until none were left except themselves.

Eighteen solutions were explored in a Carnegie-supported 1911 "Preliminary Report of the Committee of the Eugenic Section of the American Breeder's Association to Study and to Report on the Best Practical Means for Cutting Off the Defective Germ-Plasm in the Human Population." Point number eight was euthanasia.

HITLER TAKES OVER THE EUGENICS AGENDA

Shortly after taking power, Hitler passed a national law for the mandatory sterilization of certain members of the population, based on US eugenic models. This law targeted half a million people deemed physically or mentally impaired and included the feebleminded, psychotic, epileptic, blind, deaf, malformed, and chronic alcoholics. About 250,000 Germans were sterilized under these laws during the 1930s. When the Nazis opened the death camps, sterilization became less frequent, because many of those who would have been affected by this law were instead sent to the camps and killed.

The bridge from sterilization to killing was crossed quickly. Seriously malformed or retarded infants and young children were either starved to death or overdosed with drugs to end their lives. Parents and physicians received notice that the child had died of an infection or of major organ failure. But when parents and physicians protested, Hitler eventually ended this project.

The euthanasia agenda quickly grew to include misfit adults, when it came to be known under its code name "T4." Killing centers most commonly used poisonous carbon monoxide gas and sprang into action long before the killing of the Jews and others in concentration camps.

LOOKING AHEAD: THE EUGENICS AGENDA

We've been looking backwards and forwards: how eugenics got such a grip on the twentieth century and what may await us as we move further into the twenty-first. It should disturb us to see how the pieces fit together. Eugenics is the big-picture story of the challenges we face in biotechnology.

Patents

We'll see in chapter 10 that the biotech industry tried hard to prevent Congress from passing a ban on patents on human embryos. Why? As one leading legal expert wrote in an editorial comment on their strategy, there are millions of babies born in the US every year, and they want to collect royalties on them.

Genetic engineering and designer babies

Some want to do this because the technology is becoming available to make big changes in human nature – to enable you to "design" your baby. These changes could be inheritable (changes in the "germline"), so that human nature itself changes in the process. We'll look at this in more detail in chapter 7.

Cloning

Cloning technology is a key stepping stone to many of these changes. That's one reason that some biotech leaders have been fighting so hard to defend their "right" to mass-produce human embryos for experiments, and why there is growing support for the cloning of babies. In chapter 6 we'll examine the baby cloning movement, and in chapter 8 the push to make cloned human embryos for experiments.

Discrimination

Genetic information gives some people power over others. So there is a move to change the law to make it clear that no human being should be subject to genetic discrimination. But the law can do only so much. In the movie *Gattaca*, we see a society built on genetic discrimination – even while it is technically illegal.

These four themes all come together in the eugenics agenda. That's why they provide the themes for the *Manifesto on the Sanctity of Life in a Brave New World* that we signed on Capitol Hill.

The Sanctity of Life in a Brave New World: A Manifesto on Biotechnology and Human Dignity

Our children are creations, not commodities.

PRESIDENT GEORGE W. BUSH

If any one age really attains, by eugenics and scientific education, the power to make its descendants what it pleases, all men who live after are the patients of that power, slaves to the dead hand of the great planners and conditioners.

C. S. LEWIS

The Issue

The debates over human cloning have focused our attention on the significance for the human race of what has been called "the biotech century." Biotechnology raises great hopes for technological progress, but it also raises profound moral questions, since it gives us new power over our own nature. It poses in the sharpest form the question: What does it mean to be human?

Biotechnology and Moral Questions

We are thankful for the hope that biotechnology offers of new treatments for some of the most dreaded diseases. But the same technology can be used for good or ill. Scientists are already working in many countries to clone human beings, either for embryo experiments or for live birth.

In December 2002, the Raelians, a religious sect that believes the human race was cloned by space aliens, announced that a baby they called "Eve" was the first cloned human. But it is not just the fringe cults that are involved in cloning; that same month, Stanford University announced a project to create cloned embryos for medical experimentation.

Before long, scientists will also be able to intervene in human nature by making inheritable genetic changes. Biotechnology companies are already staking claims to parts of the human body through patents on human genes, cells, and other tissues for commercial use. Genetic information about the individual may make possible advances in diagnosis and treatment of disease, but it may also make those with "weaker" genes subject to discrimination along eugenic lines.

The Uniqueness of Humanity and Its Dignity

These questions have led many to believe that in biotechnology we meet *the* moral challenge of the twenty-first century. For the uniqueness of human nature is at stake. Human dignity is indivisible: the aged, the sick, the very young, those with genetic diseases — every human being is possessed of an equal dignity; any threat to the dignity of one is a threat to us all. This challenge is not simply for Christians. Jews, Muslims, and members of other faiths have voiced the same concerns. So too have millions of others who understand that humans are distinct from all other species; at every stage of life and in every condition of dependency they are intrinsically valuable and deserving of full moral respect. To argue otherwise will lead to the ultimate tyranny in which someone determines those who are deemed worthy of protection and those who are not.

Why This Must Be Addressed

As C. S. Lewis warned a half century ago in his remarkable essay *The Abolition of Man*, the new capacities of biotechnology give us power over ourselves and our own nature. But such power will always tend to turn us into commodities that have been manufactured. As we develop powers to make inheritable changes in human nature, we become controllers of every future generation.

It is therefore vital that we undertake a serious national conversation to ensure a thorough understanding of these questions, and their answers, so that our democratic institutions will be able to make prudent choices as public policy is shaped for the future.

What We Propose

We strongly favor work in biotechnology that will lead to cures for diseases and disabilities, and are excited by the promise of stem cells from adult donors and other ethical avenues of research. We see that around the world other jurisdictions have begun to develop ethical standards within which biotech can flourish. We note that Germany, which because of its Nazi past has a unique sensitivity to unethical science and medicine, has enacted laws that prohibit all cloning and other unethical biotech options. We note that the one international bioethics treaty, the European Convention on Human Rights and Biomedicine, outlaws all inheritable genetic changes and has been amended to prohibit all cloning.

We therefore seek as an urgent first step a comprehensive ban on all human cloning and inheritable genetic modification. This is imperative to prevent the birth of a generation of malformed humans (animal cloning has led to grotesque failures), and vast experimental embryo farms with millions of cloned humans.

We emphasize: All human cloning must be banned. There are those who argue that cloning can be sanctioned for medical experimentation — so-called "therapeutic" purposes. No matter what promise this might hold — all of which we note is speculative — it is morally offensive since it involves creating, killing, and harvesting one human being in the service of others. No civilized state could countenance such a practice. Moreover, if cloning for experiments is allowed, how could we ensure that a cloned embryo would not be implanted in a womb? The Department of Justice has testified that such a law would be unenforceable.

We also seek legislation to prohibit discrimination based on genetic information, which is private to the individual. We seek a wide-ranging review of the patent law to protect human dignity from the commercial use of human genes, cells, and other tissue. We believe that such public policy initiatives will help ensure the progress of ethical biotechnology while protecting the sanctity of human life.

We welcome all medical and scientific research as long as it is firmly tethered to moral truth. History teaches that whenever the two have been separated, the consequence is disaster and great suffering for humanity.

Signed by:

Carl Anderson, Supreme Knight, Knights of Columbus

Robert H. Bork, Senior Fellow, The American Enterprise Institute

Nigel M. de S. Cameron, PhD, Founding Editor, *Ethics and Medicine*;
    Dean, The Wilberforce Forum; Director, Council for Biotechnology Policy

Dr. Ben Carson, Neurosurgeon, Johns Hopkins Hospital, Department of Neurosurgery

Charles W. Colson, Chairman, The Wilberforce Forum, Prison Fellowship Ministries

Ken Connor, President, Family Research Council

Paige Comstock Cunningham, JD, Board Chair and former President, Americans United for Life

Dr. James Dobson, Focus on the Family

Dr. Maxie D. Dunnam, Asbury Theological Seminary

C. Christopher Hook, MD, Mayo Clinic

Deal W. Hudson, Editor and Publisher, *CRISIS* magazine

Dr. Henk Jochemsen, Director, Lindeboom Institute

Dr. D. James Kennedy, Senior Pastor, Coral Ridge Presbyterian Church

C. Everett Koop, MD, ScD, C. Everett Koop Institute at Dartmouth, Former US Surgeon General

Bill Kristol, Chairman, Project for the New American Century; Editor, *The Weekly Standard*

Jennifer Lahl, Executive Director, The Center for Bioethics and Culture

Dr. Richard D. Land, President, The Ethics & Religious Liberty Commission of the Southern Baptist Convention

Dr. C. Ben Mitchell, Trinity International University

R. Albert Mohler, Jr., President, The Southern Baptist Theological Seminary

Fr. Richard Neuhaus, Institute for Religion and Public Life

David Prentice, Ph.D., Professor, Life Sciences, Indiana State University

Sandy Rios, President, Concerned Women for America

Dr. William Saunders, Senior Fellow and Director, Center for Human Life & Bioethics, Family Research Council

Joni Eareckson Tada, President, Joni and Friends

Paul Weyrich, Chairman and CEO, The Free Congress Foundation

Ravi Zacharias, President, Ravi Zacharias International Ministries

God made us in his image, weak and strong, those with genes that make life easy and those with genes that can make life very hard. Our task is to treat every human being as someone worthy of the dignity God has granted each of us. What did Jesus say? If you do it to the least of these my brothers and sisters, you do it to me.

Eugenics. The word alone sends shivers up the paralyzed spine of someone like me.

Last month, I read an essay by Dr. Peter Singer, professor of bioethics at Princeton University. He noted that individuals in persistent vegetative states have no rights — since they lack self-awareness and the ability to reason, they should not be considered equal members of the human community. Peter Singer believes that people with profound retardation have no voice because they cannot make moral decisions, they are unable to rationalize, they have no volition.

Dr. Singer carries this reasoning to its logical conclusion, reminding society that the retarded and those in persistent vegetative states need no advocacy. Why speak up for individuals who are "post-persons"? He even allows for the killing of certain disabled infants up to twenty-eight days after their birth, citing they are "pre-persons." Already, his warped ethics are influencing hospital boards, hospices, and state institutions, not to mention students at Princeton University. Psalm 10:2 appears to describe well Dr. Singer's kind of ethics: "In his arrogance the wicked man hunts down the weak, who are caught in the schemes he devises."

But the Word of God gives hope to those in deep comas, suffering from locked-brain conditions, or who are retarded. Psalm 10:17 assures, "You hear, O LORD, the desire of the afflicted; you encourage them, and you listen to their cry, defending the fatherless and the oppressed." God is bending over backward to alleviate the suffering, rescue the fragile, console the dying, comfort the despairing, be a friend to, speak up for, and advocate on behalf of the weak and vulnerable. But he calls us to use *our* hands and *our* voice to speak up for, and advocate on behalf of, those who are too fragile — too small — to speak for themselves.

Our nation needs advocates for the weak. Our nation needs *heart.* Our society needs a moral center, renewed and inspired. The genuine rights of the weak, the disadvantaged, the unborn, the elderly, the cloned, the fertilized, can be safeguarded only in a society that honors life, treats humanity with respect, and shows *heart.* The Lord speaks to this lack of heart in Deuteronomy 30:16 - 20: "I command you today to love the LORD your God, to walk in his ways, and to keep his commands, decrees and laws; then you will live and increase, and the LORD your God will bless you in the land you are going to possess. But if your heart turns away and you are not obedient … I declare to you this day that you will certainly be destroyed. You will not live long in the land you are crossing the Jordan to enter and possess."

I know a little bit about heart and advocacy. Under the presidencies of Ronald Reagan and George H. W. Bush, I was appointed to the National Council on Disability. It was our responsibility to advise these two administrations, as well as Congress, on disability-related issues. I will never forget sitting on the White House lawn with other council members in the spring of 1990 as President Bush signed the Americans with Disabilities Act into law. It was a great day. This new legislation was designed to open areas of access in everything from employment to transportation. After the signing ceremony on the South Lawn, our council retired to a nearby hotel for a reception. As champagne got passed around, our council's executive director, Paul Hearne, seemed quiet. After fingering his champagne glass, he said he wanted to make an announcement.

"The ADA will mean that there will soon be mechanical lifts on busses," he said, "and ramps into restaurants … and open doors in places of employment." Paul then fell silent again. After a long moment, he continued, "But this law will *not* change the heart of the bus driver. It will not change the heart of the restaurant owner or the employer." After another long pause and with wet eyes, Paul Hearne lifted his glass in a toast: "Here's to changed hearts."

Laws and public policy reflect the heart of a country and the soul of a nation. God reminds us in Ezekiel 11:19 – 20, "I will remove from them their heart of stone and give them a heart of flesh. Then they will follow my decrees and be careful to keep my laws. They will be my people, and I will be their God."

I don't want America to move into the future with a heart of stone.

Christians are charged with the only message that can change the heart of the bus driver, restaurant owner, and employer. We are commissioned to shake salt in newspaper editorial columns, at the market, dry cleaners, PTA, or university classrooms. We have the message — and God has given us the means — to speak to ethicists who promote the idea that people are "better off dead than disabled." It is fundamentally at *this* level that a nation's heart is healed.

It's how my heart was healed when I despaired of life as a quadriplegic. Thank God there were *advocates*. There were friends and visitors, neighbors and family members who showed heart. They came into the institution where I rehabbed for two years. These dear people spoke up for and gave voice to my plight, as well as the needs of my roommates. They *advocated* for us, whether to the floor supervisor when our sheets were soiled and left unchanged, or at the University of Maryland where I needed access to second-story classrooms. These wonderful Christian friends took time to shake salt and shine light. They were God's hands … they were his advocates for one weak, depressed, paralyzed girl. And I am still feeling the repercussions of their love.

You are like these friends. You have something to say to "experts" like Dr. Singer. You have 1 Corinthians 1:20, 27 – 28, for,

> *Where is the wise man? Where is the scholar? Where is the philosopher [the so-called ethicist] of this age? Has not God made foolish the wisdom of the world? … God chose the foolish things of the world to shame the wise; God chose the weak things of the world to shame the strong. He chose the lowly things of this world and the despised things — and the things that are not — to nullify the things that are, so that no one may boast before him.*

And what do we say when the weakest are abused for the convenience of the strong? "This is what the Lord says: 'Let not the wise man boast of his wisdom or the strong man boast of his strength … but let him who boasts boast about this: that he understands and knows me, that I am the Lord, who exercises kindness, justice and righteousness on earth, for in these I delight,' declares the Lord" (Jeremiah 9:23 – 24).

You are an ambassador who represents God's kindness, justice, and righteousness on earth. You have a message that will turn a nation's heart of stone into flesh.

JONI

PART TWO

Designing Our Babies

Already we are using ultrasound and other technologies to ensure "quality control" of our unborn babies. This is eugenics in action! Many people think that if you are carrying a handicapped baby, it's a "good" reason for an abortion. And in vitro technology is being used to give us only the "best quality" embryos — and make sure that "substandard" embryos get destroyed.

Wouldn't you secretly like to clone yourself? Or your favorite relative — or sports star? So far we have only cloned animals, but around the world people are trying hard to clone people.

Did you know that you can already go a long way toward designing your own baby? You can buy sperm over the Internet and choose the kind of "father" you want. Eggs are more difficult to get, but campus newspapers all over the country carry ads for attractive, clever young women who will sell their eggs so you can pick the "mother" too. Meanwhile, science is preparing us for much more sophisticated design options, changes in the "germline" of human life itself — the ultimate genetic engineering.

This section starts with "quality control" — weeding out imperfect babies. Then we look at cloning, which could give you a choice to pick the person you want your baby to replicate. Then we look ahead to the third step in this logical process: from deselecting the defective, to copying the one you pick, to designing your baby just as you want him or her to turn out.

QUALITY CONTROL

I first met seven-year-old Rebecca at one of our Joni and Friends Family Retreats. As I sat near the dining hall, she headed up the sidewalk, her white cane clicking back and forth on the cement. Rebecca is a beautiful little girl with shiny black hair, a porcelain face, and an endearing smile. Rebecca became visually impaired at the age of four as a result of retinoblastoma, a degenerative eye disease. I sat with her during dinner and learned that she loves horses and has performed in a ballet, although now she's completely blind (she reads Braille like an expert).

Later I asked her mother about Rebecca's disability. She sighed and explained, "I had my daughter by in vitro fertilization.... Rebecca is a test-tube baby. The doctors say there's no connection, but sometimes I wonder if her in vitro procedure is at the root of it all." I wasn't too surprised by her comment. I had heard other mothers say the same. I glanced at Rebecca. *This child's handicap may have been caused by in vitro fertilization?* Rebecca bravely made her way around the Family Retreat campus, knocking her white cane against closed doors and groping along a hallway wall to get to her room. Never once did her smile dim.

Rebecca won my heart that week. So much so, that I looked up a few more facts about in vitro fertilization (IVF). One study found that "infants conceived with assisted reproductive technology were significantly more likely to have major defects than the naturally conceived infants."

I found another article in *Time* magazine that stated, "Not being able to have a baby can be heartbreaking. But having too many at once can be even worse. About 20% to 35% of IVF pregnancies produce multiple fetuses, usually twins. Having more than two or three babies at once is often a medical disaster. Babies that develop in a crowded uterus or are born too early are at risk for a lifetime of developmental problems, including mental retardation, paralysis and blindness. Trying to reduce the number of fetuses through selective abortion has its own problems, not the least of which is an increased chance of miscarriage."

In short, in vitro fertilization is fraught with problems.

But there's a bigger problem. Every day, two-thirds of the nation's 365 IVF clinics discard hundreds of human embryos. The embryos are treated like medical waste and often destroyed by means of incineration. About a third of the clinics do not dispose of them, but make them available for either adoption or scientific research. The author of one study, Arthur Caplan of the Center for Bioethics at the University of Pennsylvania, said, "There is certainly a lot more ambivalence about what embryos are than I had ever imagined before starting this study."

As far as God's Word goes, there's no ambivalence. Psalm 139:13–16 records the psalmist's passionate praise to God: "For you created my inmost being; you knit me together in my mother's womb. I praise you because I am fearfully and wonderfully made; your works are wonderful, I know that full well. My frame was not hidden from you when I was made in the secret place. When I was woven together in the depths of the earth, your eyes saw my unformed body."

What makes an embryo "fearfully and wonderfully made"? Job 33:4 states it plainly: "The Spirit of God has made me; the breath of the Almighty gives me life." A human embryo bears the unmistakable imprint of the Creator. "It is he who made us, and we are his" (Psalm 100:3). We are *his* because he has *made* us. A human embryo is the possession of God—not something to be discarded into a trash can.

That's what kept going through my mind years ago when my own quick-get-the-thermometer-stand-on-your-head effort to get pregnant never paid off. Remember that story from chapter 4? On my last visit to my infertility specialist, Dr. Fox suggested that the next step for Ken and me would be in vitro fertilization. "Would you like to move forward with that procedure?" he asked. I didn't skip a beat but shook my head no. I would not have any unborn child of mine—that's what an embryo is, an unborn child with a soul and a God-breathed origin—be discarded from a petri dish. Ken and I left Dr. Fox's office with no regrets.

Yes, I am aware that thousands of women have benefited from in vitro fertilization, resulting in thousands of children. But this does not mean there's no room for improvement. In a normal IVF procedure, over twenty embryos are created; two to four of the best are selected, and the surplus are discarded or frozen. Clinics could *significantly* limit the numbers of embryos created. The truth is, they don't see the point.

Until IVF clinics begin to make changes, I will campaign for the protection of human life and tell the facts about in vitro fertilization, such as I did on PAX TV's *Faith Under Fire*. The topic was stem cell research and the destruction of embryos. My opponent in the televised debate insisted that I should carry my view to its logical conclusion. "With your way of thinking, women who use in vitro fertilization are committing a criminal act. Would you make that procedure against the law?" he jabbed.

"Women who take part in in vitro fertilization aren't criminals," I replied. "*Everyone* has a hand in that procedure, all the way from the Supreme Court to local justices, doctors, clinicians, husbands, and wives. Our society has sanctioned IVF. I might not call it murder, but I certainly would call it 'socially approved manslaughter.'"

And if the garden-variety IVF procedure is suspect, what of all the other quality control options now available? Like I said, there are bigger problems.

Much bigger.

JONI

Eugenics, discredited by the ghastly efficiency of Hitler's Germany, has not in fact gone away. The legacy of the "better babies" movement has begun to reemerge. Its origins, as we noted, lay in the nineteenth-century idea that smart people should marry other smart people, and not "dilute the stock" by mixing their "germplasm" with that of their inferiors. This led to the idea that the "inferiors" should themselves be discouraged or prevented from reproducing. The reasons were partly economic, partly ideological, and tied in with the racism that affected so much of American life, since non-whites were regarded as inferior — a key reason for the laws in many states that forbade intermarriage across racial lines.

The second world war and the horrors of Nazi Germany seemed to discredit eugenics itself, and the civil rights movement effectively ended the laws on "miscegenation" (racial intermarriage).

So is it all over?

ABORTION, EUGENICS, AND THE DISABLED

The advent of liberal abortion after the *Roe v. Wade* decision of the Supreme Court in 1973 has reopened a door to eugenics. Many believe that while abortion for most reasons is immoral, the "good" arguments for it include preventing the birth of a child who will carry a genetic abnormality. In other words, to have an abortion because the birth of a child will interfere with your career (or your vacation plans) is plainly wrong. But to have an abortion because the child will be born handicapped may not be so bad – and, in the eyes of many people, is good. Women who have carried their children to term despite the knowledge that they are handicapped have found themselves criticized by physicians and friends alike.

As technology improves prenatal diagnosis techniques and more women take more tests, this problem will get worse. Many people assume that it is a woman's responsibility to make sure that she does not knowingly give birth to a handicapped child. Improvements in technology will greatly extend the range of genetic "problems" for which diagnosis will become possible, all the way to early baldness, obesity, and various conditions that don't arise until late in life.

A further stage in this process has been reached in the development of "pre-implantation genetic diagnosis" for couples undergoing in vitro fertilization. Many physicians fertilize more eggs than they need to initiate a pregnancy, then weed out any "substandard" embryos so that only the "good" ones get implanted.

The threat of eugenics arriving through the back door of genetic testing for disease caused a big controversy in Europe. A special group established to make recommendations to the European Commission on the use of genetic tests on newborns concluded that "genetic testing is a matter of free choice and is not to be imposed." In fact, reflecting the keen European awareness of the eugenic Nazi past, the recently written Constitution of the European Union specifically outlaws eugenics. It states: "In the field of medicine and biology the following principles must be respected ... the prohibition of eugenic practices, in particular those aiming at the selection of persons" (Article II–3).

At the same time, aware of the pressure to abort the unborn on eugenic grounds, a lobby on behalf of the disabled protests this growing practice at the United Nations. A representative of the World Federation of the Deaf-Blind told a UN hearing that "unborn children with disabilities must be protected from abortion." They declared: "Disability must not become a justification for the termination of life." A group called the Canadian Association for Living stated that prenatal genetic diagnoses are "a slippery slope toward genetic perfection."

"When Karen Coveler and her husband began trying to have a child," reports Amy Harmon in the *New York Times*, they asked for all the genetic tests possible, as she was from Ashkenazi Jewish background and that can entail some special genetic abnormalities. She was given ten tests, all of which came back negative. Still, her son Benjamin was born deaf. Karen then learned that a simple blood test could have revealed this condition during her pregnancy. Why had the hospital not done so?

"They told me that the test is not offered because the condition is not considered to be 'serious' or 'life-altering,' which I find very difficult to swallow," she commented. "It certainly has been life-altering for myself and my son." Observes the *Times*, "Too many health care providers, critics say ... choose not to inform their patients of certain tests they have deemed inappropriate, in effect making a value judgment about abortion, disabilities and risk that patients say they have a right to make for themselves."

Here we have an opposite example, which reveals the growing eugenic mindset encouraged by abortion screening. Karen says she would not have had an abortion, but would have been better able to care for her newborn. Tests for deafness often are not offered because advocates for the deaf claim that deafness is not a disease.

Where will this stop?

As the amount of genetic and other health information gleaned from simple tests continues to expand, what kind of choices will confront parents? And what kind of pressures may be put on them? The *Times* report quotes Dr. Ronald Librizzi, chief of maternal fetal medicine at Virtua Health in New Jersey, that merely *offering* a test can exert pressure on a couple to consider an abortion.

Another report in the *Times* asks the question: "What defect, if any, is reason enough to end a pregnancy that was very much wanted? Shortened limbs that could be partly treated with growth hormones? What about a life expectancy of only a few months? What about 30 years? Or a 20 per cent chance of mental retardation?" Kate Hoffman of Marblehead, Massachusetts, decided on an abortion after hearing that her much-wanted baby would have Down syndrome. They "decided that the quality of the child's life, and that of the rest of their family, would be too severely compromised."

The *Times* report continues: "Activists for the rights of the disabled say that a kind of grass-roots eugenics is evolving that will ultimately lead to greater intolerance of disabilities and less money for cures or treatments. And even some doctors who perform abortions are uncomfortable as some patients choose to quietly abort fetuses with relatively minor defects." The number of available tests is increasing. Around a dozen are regularly offered; "more than 450 conditions, including deafness, dwarfism and skin disease, can be diagnosed by testing fetal cells, with more than 100 tests added in the last year alone." Baylor College of Medicine, for example, is introducing "perhaps the largest panel" ever offered, including for $2,000 some fifty conditions that cause mental retardation.

The *Times* reports the concerns of some doctors that there is "a slippery slope from prenatal science to eugenics." One physician cites the example of a patient born with an extra finger, surgically removed when she was a child. There was a fifty-fifty chance that her children would inherit the condition. With detection through early ultrasounds, "she has terminated two pregnancies so far, despite doctors' efforts to persuade her to do otherwise."

The case of minor "defects" is especially worrying. The UK has seen a major public debate over a late abortion for a cleft palate; the case has made its way into the courts in a suit that seeks to require police to prosecute the physician involved for homicide, on the ground that this disfigurement, which can be surgically corrected, cannot be regarded as a "serious abnormality" (which the UK law requires to justify a late abortion). The case was filed by a young woman who had been born with the same condition.

EUGENICS BEFORE IMPLANTATION

The growing use of in vitro fertilization has highlighted the use of eugenic tests before embryos are even implanted. This mirrors the eugenic use of abortion, though because in some clinics it is becoming routine and does not involve the trauma of abortion, it is even more disturbing as evidence of a eugenic comeback.

From a pro-life perspective, IVF is always controversial. Many Christians (especially Roman Catholics) believe it to be unethical, however practiced. Others believe it to be a matter of conscience, but point out that some options must be ruled out: no freezing of human embryos, no creation of "extra" embryos, and no "quality control." All the embryos created should be implanted, so that the technology follows as closely as possible how things work in nature–and we do not impose our notions of quality on these tiny human lives. As we have seen, some suspect that IVF pregnancies entail higher risks of various abnormalities, and therefore pressure for "quality control" may increase to help ensure success by generating more embryos than needed, and ensuring that only the "best" ones get implanted.

An editorial in the prestigious *Journal of the American Medical Association* recently explored the ethics of pre-implantation genetic diagnosis (PGD). It notes reservations about PGD since it can be used in ways that "depart from preventive medicine"–by permitting the "diagnosis" of such factors as "selection of sex, skin color, or desirable physical characteristics" or the "designing of specific characteristics of children." The writer asks: "Is PGD the precursor of designer genetics? Where should the line be drawn?" Among the problems if this happens: "attitudes may be fostered that promote discrimination against the sick or disabled because they were not 'designed' properly prior to birth."

The technology already is in place to move from eugenic abortion, and abortion before implantation, to the design of our children (which we will consider in chapter 7).

THE SILENCE OF THE CHURCH ON IN VITRO FERTILIZATION

When did you last hear a sermon or take a Sunday school class on the rights and wrongs of test-tube babies? We have developed a mentality in the church in which we just don't talk about things like that; we treat them as private issues for parents or as technology and medicine issues on which (unlike abortion) there exists no special Christian view. Pastors have been very reluctant to get involved in any way.

Because pastors tend to ignore the issue, young couples (and sometimes singles!) go through medical referrals, visit hospitals, and take advice from physicians alone. And we now have a generation of precedent in the church for the view that so long as it does not cause abortions, reproductive technology is all right. In vitro fertilization has built a bridgehead in Christian thinking for whatever may come next.

The groundwork has been completed for yet more dramatic and damaging procedures.

Part of the challenge is in assessing something complicated. The abortion issue is, at one level, very simple: if from fertilization the tiny human being is really "one of us," then plainly his/her life may be rightly taken only in circumstances where the life of a mother might be at risk. We lack such simplicity in our attempt to make sense of in vitro as an idea. Plainly, killing embryos for research is an abortion-related act and therefore wrong. But what about freezing them? What about risking their lives in an attempt to enable pregnancy? What about the principle of technology intervening in the sexual life of a married couple? And what about the use of "donor gametes," sperm and eggs from other parties, whether genuinely "donated" and randomly selected, or chosen and purchased to produce a particular kind of child?

We need to examine three key elements in the toolkit to make sense of this and parallel issues.

First, there exist some very clear rights and wrongs – mainly, wrongs. Embryo killing, whether for research purposes or any other, is wrong. Embryo freezing is wrong. Exposing embryos to high risk is wrong (though that takes us to the question of what may constitute "acceptable risk" – for example, if it mirrors the risks facing the embryo in natural conception).

Second, we have the question of conscience. When we have counseled couples facing these questions for themselves, we have stressed the need to understand the technology and the ethical questions, and then make a decision in conscience before God. For example, what about "simple IVF," as it has been called, where a married couple is able to use their own sperm and eggs? They may decide that two eggs will be fertilized and those two embryos implanted without any "quality control" being exercised. It is a matter of conscience for the couple.

Third, there remains the question of the technology itself, whether it has its "own" values or can be considered neutral. Some Christians have taken the view that in vitro is always invasive into marriage and the procreative process. Moreover, it will tend to pressure those who use it into decisions they would have chosen not to make: what to do, for example, when the physician says the embryos need to be screened to make sure they do not carry genetic defects.

There are many technical variations on the basic in vitro idea. On the "conservative" end, that may include having the husband ejaculate his semen into a condom during intercourse, and then having the physician introduce the sperm directly into the woman's body, instead of placing the eggs in a dish. On the weirder end, it involves the commercial acquisition of gametes, sometimes on the Internet, to produce a genetically attractive child, or even the use of pre-implantation genetic diagnosis to ensure a child who could be useful for later transplants.

Another element includes "embryo adoption." This has become a popular idea, intended to rescue frozen and otherwise unwanted embryos from clinic freezers so they can be implanted in either infertile couples or couples who wish to save the lives of these tiny humans. Christians have championed this initiative in a wonderful example of the kind of practical project that enables believers to make a difference in a fallen world. But even this effort is not without problems. Couples who might hesitate to have their embryos frozen now know they might be adopted. That can never be a justification for making embryos that cannot be implanted, and then freezing them.

Because the evangelical church has uncritically absorbed in vitro techniques, millions of Christians have learned the wrong lesson at the outset of the biotech century. For in vitro contains the seeds of what is coming next:

a willingness to hazard early human life;

experimental use of embryos;

"quality control" before implantation so that only desirable human beings reach the womb;

sale and purchase of superior gametes that have eugenic appeal; and

babies conceived so their tissue can be used in later life for transplants.

Already, Christian parents have deep-frozen thousands of their embryos. These and worse practices amount to what ethicists call an "instrumentalization" of the human person—that is, treating people as things to be used for our purposes. In parallel with our use of a "manufacturing" process to bring babies into being, we have begun to treat them as "manufactured goods."

THE EUGENIC IMPERATIVE

It should surprise no one that advocates for the disabled have been among the most vocal in condemning eugenic uses of abortion. The deaf worry that deafness might come to be considered a disease (we already have examples of deaf couples seeking to use these technologies to ensure that they have deaf children). Couples who receive distressing news from prenatal screening tests find themselves under huge pressure to abort, even if the medical and nursing staff are genuinely open to their decision to continue with the pregnancy. Already, where a serious abnormality such as Down syndrome or cystic fibrosis is diagnosed, we have seen a very high level of abortions in response. Indeed, widespread testing during pregnancy has significantly reduced the incidence of these diseases by reducing the live births of children affected by them.

As more couples use IVF and related techniques to initiate pregnancy, they will face growing numbers of genetic tests (hundreds are now possible) increasingly offered as routine options – since the tests increase clinic income, prevent litigation, and improve overall "success rates."

Eugenics is on the march again, destroying the "unfit" before birth – and carrying dire implications for the dignity of the handicapped and sick. It also places unconscionable pressures on Christians who use these technologies but who yet desire to welcome children as God's gift, determined to respect the sanctity and dignity of every life.

Snowflake Parents

Bright and gregarious, happy-hearted and forward-thinking. That well describes my friends Mitzi and Jack. A strikingly handsome thirty-something couple, they nevertheless carry a quiet, relentless grief. They are childless. That is, until recently, when Mitzi instantly became six weeks pregnant. Almost overnight, her body swelled, her emotions hit the fan, and the only thing that satisfied at 2:00 a.m. was a Burrito Supreme from Taco Bell. One moment she was barren; the next, over a month pregnant.

Jack and Mitzi opted for an unusual procedure. Like most of us, they knew of thousands upon thousands of petri-dish embryos left over from in vitro fertilization procedures. They also knew that these tiny human embryos are, for the most part, destroyed. They discovered an organization called Snowflakes which rescues many of these embryos for "adoption" by couples like, well, Mitzi and Jack. They considered it their answer to prayer. A short time ago, doctors implanted several small embryos into Mitzi's uterus, hoping that one of them would make her womb his (or her!) nest. Before she knew it – voila! – Mitzi is instantly a month or so pregnant and Jack is heading out at 2:00 A.M. for another run to Taco Bell.

I called Mitzi today. She just returned from her gynecologist. "I'm having twins! I can't wait to show you the sonogram photos!" My eyes became wet at the sound of so much joy in her voice. Just a few months ago, she felt destined to be barren; today, she's buying a twin stroller.

My heart resonates with Mitzi's. At one time Ken and I also struggled with having no children. But thank the Lord for an organization like Snowflakes that provides a life-saving detour for these preborn children. It's called "embryo adoption," and it's the old, old story of redemption; that is, the "saving of many lives" by turning tragedies into triumphs. When it comes to Jack and Mitzi's adopted twins — children who are now growing to full term inside their new mother — I can't help but think of Genesis 50:20. With the help of Snowflakes, a lot of tiny ones are finding new homes, for "God intended it for good to accomplish what is now being done, the saving of many lives."

JONI

CHAPTER 6

BABY CLONING

Remember Larry? The truck driver who now sits in a wheelchair in a Arizona nursing home? The man hell-bent on either getting cured or killed? Lately he's been leaning toward that cure—but not a cure in the sense of "take two pills and I'll see you walking in the morning." Larry is hoping for a different kind of healing.

I learned about Larry's hopes for a cure when I spoke with his mother on the phone. What she said sent shivers. "Our one hope—Larry's hope —is that all these new technological advancements, all the work Christopher Reeve is doing—our hope is that with this technology, Larry will soon be on his feet."

On one hand, I hope right along with Larry. As you've already gleaned from earlier chapters, researchers are refining extraordinary new therapies using stem cells—"blank slate" cells—scraped from the nose or bone tissue of the patient. It's exciting to see what adult stem cell therapies are producing; these wonderful discoveries bring healing and hope. And I'm all for them.

But Larry's mother is thinking of a *different* kind of stem cell therapy. She's pinning all her hopes on scientists one day scraping cells from Larry's skin, extract his DNA, insert his genetic information into a woman's egg (with its nucleus removed) and—voila!—create a clone of her son. That living, human embryo would grow and, after it reaches a certain stage, technicians would harvest out its stem cells—cells that genetically match Larry's. They would then nurture and expand them into neurons which could then be replanted into Larry's mangled spinal cord. At that point, everyone would hold their breath and hope for a dream to come true.

But is cloning for cures a dream or a nightmare? Every nightmare seems to have a benign beginning—such as Larry's hope of walking—but then it slowly unfolds into a specter. Larry's mother is convinced that her

How Cloning Is Done

"Somatic cell nuclear transfer" (SCNT) produces an embryo that in every respect is identical to the embryo that results from fertilization. Only a genetic test can tell it apart from any other embryo. It is called SCNT because the nucleus of a "somatic cell" — a regular cell, like most of the cells in our body; one that is differentiated and is not linked to reproduction — is transferred into an egg that has been emptied (enucleated) of most of its genetic material. From a genetic perspective, it is almost an identical twin of the one cloned — "almost" because the mitochondria remains in the egg when its nucleus is removed. A tiny, genetically insignificant part of the genetic material of the clone comes from the egg donor.

son's best chances of walking lie with stem cells extracted from clones. More specifically, a clone of her son.

Stop there.

Do you sense anything nightmarish about that? Does it unsettle you even slightly that researchers are creating clones of human beings in order to harvest their cells?

You probably squirm at the idea but can't put your finger on exactly why. On one hand, you're all for finding a cure for diseases or for paralyzing injuries; on the other hand, something seems definitely disquieting about grappling with the stuff of human genesis. Something feels sinister about creating an entire class of human beings for the sole purpose of experimentation. You have the sense it's downright Machiavellian to clone, then kill, a human embryo merely for its parts. Isn't that exploitive? Your instincts tell you a moral compass is needed. Your Bible tells you, "There is a way that seems right to a man, but in the end it leads to death" (Proverbs 16:25).

The compass must come from someone — or something — infinitely more objective than the collective moral sensibilities of a few people or the intuitive convictions of even the majority.

You need an ethical grid that will help distinguish between good and bad, right and wrong. Something that will draw the line between a dream and a nightmare. Something that will show us who we *should* be and what we *should* be doing.

If we are to infuse Christian salt in our confused world, if we are to shine the light of Christ to people like Larry and his mother, we need to get our heads around the ethical grid.

And that grid is woven out of Genesis 1:27, for "God created man in his own image, in the image of God he created him; male and female he created them." God created man in his image. For man to create man in his image runs smack in the face of God's creative authority. Cloning is an affront to God, an open insult and purposeful offense to the Creator.

Who would have thought the future could have arrived so quickly?

Researchers are moving forward at jet-blast speed, fueled by a bio-tech industry anxious for profits and venture capitalists looking for a robust return on investment. Larry and his mother are benign players in a global medical drama that is copying, replicating, and genetically manipulating human beings at a breakneck pace.

This isn't space-age wacko science fiction talk.
It's a nightmare looming on the horizon.
And it's coming our way.

JONI

Is Cloning Illegal?

Some countries have already banned cloning, including Canada, France, Australia, Norway, and Germany. All have comprehensive cloning bans, making it illegal to clone human embryos for any purposes, either for experiments or to produce cloned babies. In a handful of countries such experiments are permitted. In the United Kingdom, cloning experiments are encouraged and funded by the government; but experimenters are required to kill the embryos, because it remains illegal to produce cloned babies.

In the United States, vigorous debates have taken place about the best approach to take. No federal law currently exists, although the Food and Drug Administration has said that it has the authority and the will to prevent the birth of cloned babies. Some states have banned all cloning, while a small number allow cloning for experiments. California has raised $3 billion dollars in a ballot to fund "stem cell research," which includes cloning and killing human embryos.

On Valentine's Day, 2002, a simple headline announced the birth of a kitten to the world: "Pet cloning could be just a whisker away." Researchers in Texas had successfully cloned a cat. Eighty-six other kitten embryos died in the process, but "CC" survived. With funding from a wealthy couple who originally wanted to clone their dog, the first example of pet cloning had succeeded. If you have seen the Schwarzenegger movie *The Sixth Day*, you will remember its vision of a world in which pet cloning had become standard.

The success of pet cloning certainly brings the cloning of people one giant step nearer.

CRAZY CLONERS

The UFO man

Rael is a strange man. He wears a flowing white robe and keeps his hair long. He used to be a sports writer and drive race cars, but thirty years ago he changed tracks and founded a sect—a sect with a difference.

Raelians, as his followers are called, believe in UFOs. They believe that creatures from space visited the earth long ago and started human life. How did they do it? By cloning. So when Rael and his followers heard the news that a sheep had been cloned, they knew their big opportunity had come.

First they began to issue press releases saying that they favored cloning babies. Then they got invited to testify at hearings in Congress so they could make their case. Rael and his scientist colleague, Brigitte Boisillier, appeared on our TV screens and in the press week after week. Finally, at the close of 2002, they carried off their biggest coup. They claimed that they had engineered the birth of the first cloned baby. They claimed they would arrange independent proof, through a well-known science journalist. For a few days, their press conferences seemed like the biggest news story in the world—until they changed their mind. They used various excuses to cancel the "proof" process.

In interviews Rael himself told the world that Brigitte Boisillier was a remarkable woman; either she had really cloned a baby, or she had convinced the world that she had.

Let Clonaid Clone *You!*

Welcome to CLONAID™—the first human cloning company! CLONAID™ was founded in February 1997 by Rael, the leader of the Raelian Movement, an international religious organization, which claims that a human extraterrestrial race, called the Elohim, used DNA and genetic engineering to scientifically create all life on Earth.

CLONAID.COM

One reporter wrote: "Either this was one of the most momentous announcements of all time or it was a cheap gimmick designed to garner maximum publicity for an outlandish cult that believes in aliens from outer space. It might be both."

It was, of course, one of the biggest hoaxes ever. The world press had made sure we all stayed glued to the story. And the Raelians established themselves (for a short while, anyway) as the best-known sect on the planet.

The Strange Dr. Seed

Besides the Raelians, some scientists say they are at work on the first human clone. Back in 1998 a man named Dr. Richard Seed appeared on Chicago television to announce that he would be the first to clone a baby. Everyone wondered if that could be his real name! No one in the scientific community took him seriously, partly because of his strange appearance and partly because he had a background in physics rather than biology. But the public responded so strongly that President Bill Clinton came out of the White House to reassure Americans that Dr. Seed would not be allowed to succeed. Cloning babies would be stopped.

Dr. Seed remained defiant. "I happen to disagree with the president rather strongly," he said. Then he sketched out his view of technology and the future. "I believe man will develop the technology and science and the capability to have an indefinite life span and what goes with that is the capability to have an unlimited knowledge. It's the next step from animal cloning."

Dr. Seed's Pro-Cloning Case

Cloning is a legitimate treatment of infertility.

Cloning can be used to replace a lost loved one with a twin; for example, a child tragically killed in a car accident.

Human cloning will unleash a torrent of research that will benefit mankind by vastly increasing our knowledge of medicine and biology.

Human cloning can take a 65-year-old and turn the age of that person back to zero – to the one-cell stage. It is not unreasonable to expect that in the future we can turn the age of the 65-year-old back to 25!

Bioethicists are nay-sayers. The bioethicist movement started in the 1970s. For the most part, the role of bioethicists is to say no to change and to resist progress. Historically, they have been wrong over and over again.

Summary by Human Cloning Foundation, humancloning.org

More Rogue Scientists

The Raelians and Dr. Seed are not alone in wanting to clone babies. Severino Antinori is a leading Italian ob-gyn and a specialist in in vitro fertilization – test-tube babies – and it has made him famous around the world. To be precise, he is not just famous; he is notorious, primarily because he has enabled women well past childbearing age to bear children. The oldest, so far, is a sixty-four-year-old grandmother.

Nobel Laureate Supports Cloning

"James Watson, one of the discoverers of the secret of DNA half a century ago, is backing the right of Severino Antinori, the maverick Italian scientist, to create a human clone. He told *The Independent* on Sunday that he had no ethical or scientific objections to scientists trying to create clones.... 'I'm not going to worry about him. If the first clone is born, it's not going to kill the Earth.' "

Dr. Antinori had been working with an American scientist, Professor Panos Zavos. They have testified, made speeches, and appeared on television talk shows to make their case in favor of cloning. They have been telling the world that they are at work in their labs, preparing the way for the birth of the first cloned babies. Antinori and Zavos have told the press they are no longer working together, but are now collaborating with colleagues in other countries. While it is hard to know where the truth lies, one thing seems certain: these pro-cloning people love being in the news!

In August, 2002, Zavos announced that he had seven couples ready to begin cloning procedures. Then he produced Bill and Kathy (with their identities disguised) to prove it. They planned to use Kathy's DNA, so the clone would be her "twin sister" as well as her daughter.

NOT-SO-CRAZY CLONERS

Pro-Cloners Who Can't Be So Easily Dismissed

It would be easy to get the impression that only crazy people, such as UFO cultists and publicity-seeking rogue scientists, want to clone babies. And when the media focuses on them and their antics, they certainly make good television! Someone has said that not one single vote exists on Capitol Hill in favor of cloning babies.

But things are not quite so simple.

Side by side with the crazies is a growing group of academics in the bioethics and medical communities who *do* favor cloning. While they know it may be some time before safety issues get resolved, they are already making their case that baby cloning should be permitted.

This group includes Dr. Greg Pence, medical school ethics professor from Alabama and author of a manifesto in favor of cloning: *Who's Afraid of Human Cloning?* Another prominent pro-cloner, Texas law professor Dr. John Robertson, carries influence with many physicians and scientists.

Some celebrities have joined the bandwagon, including Arnold Schwarzenegger, now governor of California. Mr. Schwarzenegger once starred in a memorable cloning movie, *The Sixth Day*, and in real life has been quoted as saying, "I would go for it. I would have been cloned."

One of the most disturbing proponents is British philosopher Mary Warnock. Twenty years ago, after in vitro fertilization first made its appearance, she was asked to chair a commission to help shape the law regarding the practice. Today she is quoted as saying, "I can't see any reason to believe that in ten or twenty years' time there won't be human cloning anywhere in the world.... It would not be the end of the world if a man was cloned." Lady Warnock is one of the most influential voices in the world of biotech policy.

The In Vitro Doctors Keep Their Options Open

The in vitro doctors' organization is called the American Society for Reproductive Medicine (the ASRM). If one day baby cloning is successful and becomes legal, these are the people who would add cloning to their list of options for anyone who wishes to take advantage of the new baby-making technology. And the evidence suggests that they are wide open to the possibility.

Officially the ASRM is against baby cloning. Its representatives have so testified before Congress, and the society has a clear anti-cloning statement on its website. But *why* is it against baby cloning? Look at what this group has said: "We have reviewed the scientific data ... given the current state of knowledge, any attempt at human cloning would be scientifically inappropriate and thus unethical."

You have to look twice to realize just what the ASRM's position is. Why is baby cloning unethical? Because it is "scientifically inappropriate." And why is it scientifically inappropriate? The *only* reason the ASRM so far opposes baby cloning is that it is not—at the moment—"safe." It may harm babies and also the women who carry them in their wombs. We need more tests on animals, more experiments, before it can become "scientifically appropriate." Once it does, all of a sudden, it will become "ethical."

In fact, their public statements say nothing about opposing cloning in principle. So while they like to hear their "anti-cloning" stance quoted, their actual position is identical to that of people like bioethics professor Gregory Pence. He opposes cloning too—at the moment, when it seems too risky. But he is also one of cloning's leading defenders.

The only difference is that he *likes* people to think he is pro-cloning. We saw earlier in this chapter that he has written a book to argue his case. As a professor, he makes speeches, writes books, and generally enjoys playing the role of gadfly as he debates his case.

The in vitro doctors want us to think of them as responsible. They continually point to their anti-cloning stance. But in fact they agree with Dr. Pence. They have no problem with baby cloning in principle. Once it is "safe," they plan to start cloning babies to order.

WHAT CLONING IS AND WHAT IT ISN'T

The Dolly Story

It's hard to remember now what a big story cloning was back in 1997. Dolly the sheep stared at us from TV screens and the covers of news magazines. The media ran specials to remind us of our high school biology so we could better understand the story. It remained the lead story for a long time.

Dolly's cloning took everyone by surprise. To that point cloning was a science fiction idea that scientists thought might one day become possible, but not for many years. The technique used by the scientists who cloned Dolly so surprised some experts that they thought it must have been a fluke or a fraud. They thought the technique just couldn't have worked, partly because it was too simple.

How Does Cloning Work?

The goal of cloning is to make mammals—including, perhaps, human beings—that are identical to others already born. The technique used to clone Dolly is called "somatic cell nuclear transfer." How does it work?

When mammals (including humans!) reproduce, two gametes are involved: the egg from the female, and the sperm from the male. The sperm penetrates the egg and fertilizes it so it becomes a tiny new member of the species. Cloning completely alters the procedure. It is called "asexual" reproduction, since it involves neither sexual relations between male and female, nor the union of sperm and egg. (While in vitro fertilization does not involve sexual relations, it still depends on the fertilization of an egg with sperm, in a lab.)

Cloning creates a new member of the species basically by splitting off an identical twin from an existing member of the species. The method takes the genetic material from a cell of one animal (in Dolly's case, from the skin of the udder of the sheep being copied), and injects it into an unfertilized egg from which most of the genetic material has been removed. When this new genetic stuff is introduced to the empty egg, the latter is persuaded (using chemicals and electricity) to behave like an egg that has been fertilized.

In Dolly's case, 277 eggs were fertilized. Only one led to a reasonably healthy, live-born baby lamb. But because all you need to clone is genetic material from an adult cell and a supply of eggs, large numbers of identical clones can be produced. Dolly was reasonably healthy, but not completely. In the end she had to be put to death.

Dolly's Obituary

She was created by biotechnicians, debated by theologians and finally put to sleep by veterinarians. Now Dolly the sheep has been stuffed by taxidermists and put on display before the public.

REUTERS NEWS SERVICE

One of the loudest voices against cloning babies has been Rudolph Jaenisch of the Massachusetts Institute of Technology, perhaps the world's leading expert on animal cloning. He says that cloning a human "would probably damage more than 1,000 of its genes ... so that even normal-looking clones would harbour hidden health problems." He draws these conclusions from studies of the thousands of animals that have been cloned. In cloned mice, one in twenty-five genes gets damaged. And the result? "Recent studies showing premature death, pneumonia, liver failure, and obesity in aging cloned mice could be a consequence."

Indeed, protests have come from animal rights activists about the pain and suffering this is causing cloned animals. "Deaths and deformities in cloned animals are the norm, not the exception, and these studies make plain once again that these creatures are suffering terribly in the process," said Wayne Pacelle of the Humane Society of the United States.

Are There "Good Arguments" for Cloning?

We have no lack of bad arguments and weird people who argue in favor of cloning. Remember the bizarre Ted Williams story? A family fight developed when the baseball great's son had his father's body frozen so they could clone him once the technology had been perfected.

People wish to replicate their loved ones. A couple wants to clone one of themselves. Once cloning starts, it is hard to see how we will ever stop it. It will go well beyond infertility (always used as the best-case argument, since we have so much sympathy for the infertile). We shall not have to wait long before we start cloning celebrities. How many couples would really like to have as their child the genetic twin of their favorite sports or movie or singing star? Or maybe their favorite preacher?

If that sounds unlikely, don't forget that Bill and Kathy – Panos Zavos's guinea-pig couple who, he says, will be the first Americans to have a cloned baby – say they are Christians and that this is God's plan for them. "I think God really wants us to do this," they said to Connie Chung on CNN. "I can't imagine any reason why we haven't had a child, other than this is what we were meant to do."

Let's look at some of the "good cases" that involve no celebrities, no mass cloning of Hitlers or Einsteins. And let's assume that cloning proves safe. What about an infertile couple who, like Dr. Zavos's Bill and Kathy, choose cloning over in vitro? Bill and Kathy plan to clone Kathy. They could have chosen to clone Bill. Either way would work.

Some people have argued that cloning is actually preferable to in vitro that uses "donor gametes" – sperm and egg from outside the marriage – as it means the child is genetically related to at least one parent. However, this presents a new problem: the cloned "daughter" (in this case) is *very* closely related – too closely. In fact, she is her "mother's" biological sister. She is actually the biological daughter, not of Bill and Kathy at all, but of Kathy's parents. As Kathy sees her "daughter" growing up as the spitting image of herself, it is plain that the family will go through some very strange experiences. How will the daughter differentiate herself from her mother, who is essentially the same as her? And how will Bill feel as he watches the woman he fell in love with (his wife) grow up as his daughter? The complications boggle the mind, and the ensuing family and personal dysfunctions are virtually assured. The notion that cloning is simply "an alternative to in vitro" is ridiculous. It's a recipe for a very strange family life, indeed.

The other "good argument" concerns the case of a child who dies and parents who want to "replace" the child with a clone. Once again, our hearts go out to people who have to face such tragedy. It is more difficult to say no to such a scenario than to any other situation. One time when the Raelians testified at a congressional hearing, they read a tragic letter from a couple whose child had died and whom they wanted to clone—though the argument backfired when one of the members of Congress pointed out that, according to the letter, the child had actually died of a genetic disorder. So if he were cloned, his twin would have the same problems and could die in just the same way.

Growing Up in Counseling

I once sat on ABC's *Nightline*, facing a pro-cloning bioethics expert who offered the following example: What about a couple whose child dies, and who want to clone that child for their next baby? If the child does not die of a genetic disorder, they could use cloning to have his or her "twin," who would have every chance of being healthy. The anchor turned to me and asked me to comment. I asked a question: Who speaks for the child? We have so much sympathy for the parents. But the key moral question is about the child-to-be and his or her well-being. I suggested that this child would grow up in counseling, for early on this little child would realize that he or she is a copy of another child. Whether they share the same room, or clothes, or toys, or even have different ones, growing up is all about comparisons with and memories of someone else — not about this new life, this fresh person, who should exist and know that he or she exists for his or her own sake. By all means, let's have sympathy for the parents; but what about the child? "Is that a good example of cloning?" I quipped; "Give me a bad one!" And the anchor turned to the bioethics expert and said, "Dr. Cameron has a good point, doesn't he?"

NIGEL CAMERON

So Why Shouldn't We?

Shortly after the announcement of Dolly's cloning, a leading Christian physician picked up the phone and began calling his friends. "I know this is wrong," he said. "We can't let them do this to people. But I'm just not sure *why*. Can you tell me?"

Something deep down in most of us "just knows" this isn't right, that we shouldn't be making people, copying people, mass-producing people. Dr. Leon Kass, who chaired the President's Council on Bioethics, has called it "repugnance," and says we are wise to feel that way. But we have to explain *why*.

If we ask the question like that, many of us will not find it easy to answer. "Give me three reasons why cloning is wrong." What might they be?

Before we list some responses, we have to get our bearings. As we have seen, it isn't always easy to get inside arguments about something as vital but as unusual as making babies. We know that abortion is wrong, and anything that kills or threatens embryos and fetuses (and newborns!) must therefore be wrong. But these technologies have crept up on us while we looked the other way.

Plainly, at the moment, cloning is a very dangerous technology. If it is proved to work in human beings, it will have come at the cost of countless experimental embryos. If it follows the pattern of Dolly, it will lead to deformed fetuses and newborns that die. That is why many scientists and the fertility doctors' organization currently oppose cloning babies. But what if we woke up tomorrow and someone had solved the technical problems? What if cloning didn't threaten embryos and women anymore? Would it still be wrong?

Consider God's design for new people. It starts with sexual intercourse in the context of marriage. Part of the beauty of that design is how it separates our babies from us. We never know whether a given act of sex will result in conception. And even though we may pick our marriage partners partly because we like the idea of kids who resemble them, there is a genetic mystery at work—unbelievers would call it a lottery!—that mixes up the genes in incredibly complex ways. You may marry a tall, handsome, blonde guy and have a baby boy who resembles that uncle of his you never did get to meet. We don't control the genetic mix. So we don't *design* our children; they are never "products" that we have planned or "commodities" we have obtained. They are, right from the start, *other people*, whom we care for and love but never own.

So what's wrong with cloning?

Cloning flips us into a whole different way of relating to children. We pick the genes we like—mine, yours, a celebrity's—and choose whose "twin" our next baby will be. The dividing line between "having a baby" and "buying a product" becomes much thinner and may get erased altogether.

We already know a lot about the life that will unfold, because someone has lived its genes before. Of course, we know that identical twins do not lead identical lives. But many things remain the same for them, even if they are raised apart—and will therefore be the same with a clone. While with twins the future remains unknown, as they remain the same age, with a clone we could have detailed knowledge of what the future might bring. We sample this experience as we look at our parents and realize how much we grow like them. But with a clone it will be *much* stronger.

Very confused family relationships will unfold. We saw how this might work with Kathy and Bill, Dr. Zavos's cloning couple. They plan to clone Kathy. Their baby will be her identical twin. Their "daughter" will be Bill's sister-in-law. Her real parents will be Kathy's parents. It is naive to believe that all this will make no difference as the little girl grows up. Imagine the strains in the family as she goes through adolescence, or if the marriage comes under pressure.

We are all a blend of nature and nurture. The nature comes from our genes; the nurture from our experience. Pro-cloners sometimes use this fact to suggest that we needn't worry too much. But it also works the other way. Kathy and Bill will feel *very* tempted to copy key experiences from Kathy's early life to make sure that their "daughter" turns out like Kathy (which is presumably why they wanted to clone her in the first place).

Imagine the pressure when people start cloning celebrities. Perhaps you spend your savings so you can have as your next child a clone of a famous ball player (maybe Ted Williams). You will be very interested in how the guy you picked and cloned was raised. If he spends his spare time watching TV or playing chess, he is likely to waste his ball-playing talent. So you read up on the young Ted Williams and see how he spent his time, what key experiences he had. (If you saw the movie, *The Boys from Brazil*, you will get the point. They cloned Hitler, and then killed all the little boys' dads at the age that Hitler's dad died. That's an extreme example, but it makes the point.) There will be books with titles like *Raising Your Clone for Dummies* to help you get it right. After all that investment in the nature, you don't want to mess up the nurture, do you?

At the Movies

The Boys from Brazil, a thriller made in 1978, starred Gregory Peck as Josef Mengele. Directed by Franklin Schaffner, it is credited with reawakening interest in Nazi fugitives in South America. Originally rated an R, it is mild by comparison with some contemporary R ratings. The most disturbing piece occurs toward the end; most of those who have seen it have never forgotten the dogs.

It develops a simple theme: Nazis clone Hitler and raise their Hitler clones to take over the world. The film features superior plot and dialog (and casting) and, unlike some other movies (like the silly *Multiplicity*), it understands cloning. The bad guys take great pains to replicate the conditions of Hitler's childhood in their little Hitlers, all the way to killing their fathers when the boys reach the age Hitler was when his own father died.

Columbia released *The Sixth Day* in 2001, starring Arnold Schwarzenegger. The plot gets a little complicated, but the basic idea features a world in which pet cloning is the norm, but human cloning remains illegal. The "sixth day" of the title comes from Genesis 1 (lost on many audiences), and refers to a law that makes cloning illegal—and has led the Supreme Court to require the death of a clone.

When "CC," the cat, was cloned in 2002—the first pet cloning—the story began to seem a little more credible. Putting cloned people to death seems a curious way to deal with the issue, but it draws attention to its significance.

And then what do you do when your little Ted Williams look-alike falls off his bike at the age of four, breaks his leg badly, and ever after walks with a limp? Do you ask for your money back?

Cloning dehumanizes us and treats people like things.

What Will Happen If We Clone?

Some pro-cloners talk as if we can allow these techniques to be used in special cases, like infertility, and prevent their use for other purposes. Not likely!

Once this technology gets perfected, people around the world will use it for many purposes. Infertile couples will certainly use it. There will most certainly be special interest from gays and lesbians. Individuals and couples will use it to copy people for every possible reason. Some will copy themselves or their loved ones. Some will copy their parents, aunts, or uncles.

Use your imagination. Legacies will be tied to a requirement that grandchildren clone their deceased grandparents. Groups of people—maybe like the Raelians—will clone their leaders or their heroes. Leaders like Saddam Hussein and Nicolae Ceaucescu, who plan long-term for their nations and expect to remain in power for decades, might clone themselves in large numbers.

Meanwhile, in the "free world," we will witness the spectacle of celebrity cloning—hundreds, thousands, of Michael Jordans, Orlando Blooms, and Gwyneth Paltrows—whoever is considered the biggest star of the day, assuming they agree to have their genes used—and perhaps even if they don't. A whole new kind of crime could emerge of stealing DNA ... not hard to do.

What would it be like to be one of a hundred, or ten thousand, "identical twins," all of different ages, all copied from someone famous? It's a weird sci-fi scenario, but if this technology takes hold, it looks inevitable.

During debates on this issue, I've been scoffed at, called an alarmist, and pooh-poohed. "This is progress; this is technology that will give

Clonaid™: New Cloning Services

- If you are a sterile couple with no more hope of having the child you dream of,
- If you are a homosexual couple with a profound desire to have a child carrying your own genes,
- If you are infected with the HIV virus and you would like to have a child carrying your own genes without passing on the virus to the baby or to your partner,
- If you just lost a beloved family member and would like to see an identical twin of him/her live again,
- If you want to be cloned, whatever your reasons may be, then CLONAID™ has the right program for you.

Clonaid.com

us cures in this generation. How can you, with a clear conscience, use such scare tactics, whipping up unfounded fears in people's minds? You belong in the past, not the future!"

Maybe *they* belong in the past—the recent past. My opponents in those debates need a history lesson. Remember what happened just a little over fifty years ago in Nazi Germany. When medical teams began their insidious experiments, the first to be carted away in the dark, in the middle of the night, were the mentally defective. Researchers—or at least their cohorts—entered the hallways of mental institutions to whisk away disabled people. But not just *any* disabled people. Nazi medical teams singled out mentally handicapped individuals who had no visitors, no family members, no advocates, and no friends to speak up for them. After many months when still no one spoke up, medical teams then carted away physically disabled people.

Then gypsies.

Then Jews.

This is the nightmare. Sin left unchecked always grows darker. Jeremiah 17:9 says, "The heart is deceitful above all things and beyond cure. Who can understand it?"

It's a history lesson cloning advocates need to learn.

Larry, with his crushed lungs and snapped spinal cord, lies exposed in a society that thinks nothing of creating a class of human beings for medical experimentation. Larry and millions like him remain vulnerable in a culture that keeps redrawing the line of "viability" for a human being. Already our society has violated human embryos; little wonder we've become calloused about cloning them. And the difference between killing or cloning an embryo and discarding people with disabilities is only a matter of degree.

Remember, evil left unchecked has a way of becoming more evil.

As a friend in a wheelchair has said, "This is not a slide down the slippery slope. This is downhill skiing. And the way to stop it is to draw the line *right now*. Not just because that line is right, but because the very notion of drawing lines is at stake." The rights of the weak, of people like Larry in his wheelchair, are safeguarded only in a society that honors life.

That's why I must speak up from my wheelchair. We need friends like you to speak up and speak out too. We even need those who might only "visit" this topic of cloning. Whether human beings are quadriplegics or clones, we must push the line back to the Word of God. All it takes is courage and wisdom.

For "wisdom will save you from the ways of wicked men, from men whose words are perverse, who leave the straight paths to walk in dark ways, who delight in doing wrong and rejoice in the perverseness of evil, whose paths are crooked and who are devious in their ways" (Proverbs 2:12–15).

And if anyone wants to know, Larry and I have a much better chance of walking using *adult* stem cell therapies. More on that a little later.

JONI

CHAPTER 7

DESIGNER BABIES

I'm a quadriplegic. I know my limits. You'll never strap me to an able-bodied parachute-jumper to go skydiving. You'll never catch me following my quad-friend Becki into the ocean deep to scuba dive the Caribbean Sea. I will never go bungee jumping in my wheelchair, nor be lowered into a cave. I don't care how many disabled people are joining handicap equestrian clubs, I will *not* be talked into getting up on a horse. None of that Evel Knievel stuff in my power wheelchair, thank you.

Not one to go to extremes, I'm the type who enjoys watching other people free-fall, bungee jump, scuba dive, and horseback ride. The other evening I was reading a book about Sir Edmund Hillary's ascent to the top of Mt. Everest. In 1953, the world considered his climb a global extreme. One world-class climber wrote, "Humans must constantly push their limits—if something's broken, we fix it; if there's a problem, we must solve it; if there's an ocean, we cross it; if there's a mountain, we must climb it." It's the principle behind all the extreme television programs so popular these days. There's the *Extreme Home Improvement* show, *Extreme Surfing*, and *Extreme Skateboarding*.

The most popular of all is *Extreme Makeover*, where dowdy women and double-chinned men subject themselves to a complete body makeover. We're not talking a little bit of Revlon blush, an eye lift, and a hairpiece; we're talking hundreds of thousands of dollars spent in reconstructing jaws, liposuctioning hips, redesigning chins, and enhancing breasts and buttocks. One woman, interviewed afterward, enthused, "It's amazing! If you don't like your body, you can redesign it!" When she stepped from behind the curtain to show her friends and family her extreme makeover, everyone gasped in delight. The few who seemed a little disapproving were soon silenced. Who could argue with someone's preference to improve his or her life?

We seem to be grabbing at technology as though it were a magic wand, designing our breasts and backsides, brains, broken genes, and babies, all in one breath.

These are the days of global extremes. Plus, we are a global community. We live in a smaller world where people with river blindness in West Africa might well be called our neighbors. It begs the question: What responsibility does the woman who spends $450,000 on a new face and figure have toward a child in Albania who will die for want of a simple surgery on her esophagus? And not only the woman—what responsibilities lie with doctors and technicians? What about investors and research institutes, pharmaceutical companies and plastic surgery centers?

Who *are* our neighbors? How should we triage not only our wealth, but our technology?

Almighty God scrutinizes what we do with our wealth and subsequent technological advancements, for he tells us in Hebrews 4:13, "Nothing in all creation is hidden from God's sight. Everything is uncovered and laid bare before the eyes of him to whom we must give account." What we think about biotechnology—what we decide, and how we persuade or advise others—*counts* before God.

Matthew 12:36-37 warns, "But I tell you that men will have to give account on the day of judgment for every careless word they have spoken. For by your words you will be acquitted, and by your words you will be condemned."

If there's an ocean, cross it; if there's a mountain, climb it. But designing babies? Enhancing genetic performance? Selecting the fetus with potentially the best brains?

I don't think so.

Let's leave the extremes to the surfboarders. May God grant us the power to change the things we can, grace to accept the things we can't, and the wisdom to know the difference.

JONI

We have already seen the legacy of eugenics in America and in Germany, and observed the beginnings of a new eugenics as "quality control" screens out the handicapped—whether in the lab as test-tube babies are conceived, or through the abortion of the less-than-perfect. We also saw how the cloning of babies is becoming technically possible, and that some influential voices support the practice.

But destroying the inferior, and copying those whom we like, amount only to steps on the way to the real goal of eugenics: superior people who reflect our preferences. That is, real "designer babies." New technologies are coming together to make this possible. And to see how this approach is already getting under our skin, we come back to a technology we have already grown used to. Whether or not in vitro fertilization is ever right, it is increasingly being used in ways that take us straight back to eugenics – and take us forward to a much more sophisticated eugenics in the years to come.

CHOOSING OUR BABIES

The choices that test-tube baby technology makes possible are already facing people with terrible dilemmas . . . and temptations. Sharla Miller and her husband had three sons: Anthony, Alec, and Ashton.

"They fish, hunt, and do all that stuff with their dad," she says. "I go along, not necessarily enjoying it, but to be part of the family." So when she wanted to have another child, she determined it had to be a girl. With her husband Shane, she visited a California fertility clinic.

"Several medical procedures and $25,000 later, Miller got what she had wished for, times two. She is due to deliver twin girls." They created four more healthy female embryos, and seven more boys. They have frozen them while they work out what to do with them.

Sometimes things go terribly wrong. "Laura Howard was hoping her trip to a fertility specialist would make her dream of a child with the man she loves come true. But as she left the office, the doctor suddenly ran out to the lobby and called her back. There was a grave mistake. Instead of being inseminated with the sperm of her fiancé, she received a vial of semen from another man." Two weeks later she was confirmed pregnant. "'I don't sleep. I am always stressed,' Howard said. 'My fiancé is very distraught. He had no intentions of raising someone else's child.'"

China's Missing Girls

China is missing girls – forty to sixty million of them – which will leave an equal number of young Chinese men without wives. Chinese couples, allowed to have only one or two children, abort girls in the womb in order to try for boys. Boys are preferred for traditional cultural reasons, because they support their parents in their old age (girls become part of their husbands' families when they marry), because they extend the family line, and because in rural areas, they can perform more labor.

Between 117 and 119 boys are now born in China for every 100 girls, when 105 boys should be born for every 100 girls (Mother Nature prefers boys by 5 percent). The Chinese government has announced plans to eliminate the new disparity between male and female births by 2010, just five years away.

The London *Financial Times* reports on the polarized public debate that new technology is producing. Going beyond the screening out of diseases, "the discovery of genes linked with traits such as aggression and sexual orientation have raised fears of a reawakening of eugenic policies aimed at improving the gene pool." Helena Kennedy, chair of the UK's Human Genetics Commission, "has warned against the creation of a genetic underclass that is unable to obtain medical insurance and the possibility of discrimination against people who refuse to terminate handicapped babies."

Britain's Human Fertilisation and Embryology Authority felt compelled to deny a report that parents would be able to choose such features as hair or eye color. In an admission that "ethics" is also under review, the spokeswoman said: "It's such a fast-moving area and they will look at how much the science has advanced as well as looking at whether the ethical and legal sides have moved on." The idea that the "ethical side" is "moving on," like the science, says more than she intended about the British approach, the most "liberal" in the free world.

US News and World Report carried a report under the title "Our Biotech Bodies, Ourselves," asking the question: "What if, by taking a drug, you could possess an IQ of 250? Or by tinkering with your genes, you could have the athletic prowess of a decathlete? Or by injecting yourself with stem cells, live to be 160? Would you do it? Would these enhancements make you less human?"

The report continues: "In a speech last year before a gathering of enhancement advocates, William Sims Bainbridge, a deputy director at the National Science Foundation who studies the societal impact of technology, warned that 'scientists may be forced into rebellion in order to carry out research prohibited unnecessarily by powerful institutions.'"

As the *US News and World Report* shows us, while the "designer baby" question begins with the screening of in vitro embryos and unborn babies for serious genetic disease, it goes on ... and on ... and on. First we have trivial uses of the screening technology (like the woman who aborted two babies because they had an extra finger). Next, we have "positive" uses of it, like wanting a boy of red hair or a sunny disposition. Then, as new technologies come on stream, we start making serious changes in human nature.

In Vitro Fertilization: The Reproductive Genie Out of the Test Tube

The birth of Louise Brown in England in 1978, the world's first test-tube baby, triggered a worldwide debate about two key issues—in vitro itself, and back of that, whether human embryos should be used for experiments. Only through years of experiments on human embryos had Louise Brown become possible.

Most of the ethics debate naturally focused on the use of embryos for experiments that would end in their death (we discuss this in the next chapter). There was little discussion of the techniques themselves, as a means of enabling women to have babies after fertilization in the lab—especially not among evangelicals. The Roman Catholic church gave guidance to its members, and criticized any use of the technology. Since the Catholic church does not approve of most forms of contraception, such a stance did not prove a great surprise and suggested to many evangelicals that this was not an issue for them. The wide-spread evangelical approval of contraceptives that do not kill embryos (some techniques do) could include an approval for in vitro. But for a technology with such enormous implications – including for Christian couples struggling with infertility and other problems, such as inherited disease – the near silence of the evangelical church was a disaster. Tens of thousands of Christians have made use of these technologies, often without any idea of the serious ethical issues at stake.

Surrogacy at the Church Door

Believers have been left to their own devices. I remember speaking in a church on Sanctity of Life Sunday about test-tube babies, and being met at the door by a couple who felt anxious to introduce me to her sister, acting as a surrogate mother, heavily pregnant with their child. I remember leaving our own church worship service one Sunday and being asked urgently by someone I barely knew to call his daughter and her husband that afternoon, as the next morning she would be taken into the hospital to begin the process of in vitro. He said she felt badly about it, but was being pushed into it by her husband. I did call them; we had a long discussion and they decided to cancel the treatment. Another Sunday I was to be guest speaker and someone "warned" me that the pastor's children had all been in vitro babies. The list goes on and on.

NIGEL CAMERON

And the problem lying behind all of these examples is not that in vitro is necessarily wrong, but that few have been thinking about whether and when and why it might be right. A vast revolution has taken place in the way in which many families (and also singles) are enabled to have children, and the evangelical church has consistently avoided facing the question and inquiring and advising appropriately. As a sign of how well we shall be able to cope with the next stages in this continuing revolution in biotech and human dignity, it is not encouraging.

One huge problem is that embryos are observed and evaluated, and only "good" ones get implanted – the ones seen to have the best chance of success. Any with diagnosable genetic or other problems are destroyed. So in vitro provides the context for a dramatic "quality control" exercise at the start of human life.

The other basic problem is that of the "spare" embryos. If a group of embryos is fertilized, what of the others – "good" or otherwise – that do not get implanted? The custom has been to freeze them and maintain them in case the couple chooses to have another in vitro pregnancy – either because this one fails, or they decide to have more children. Thus they avoid the costly and unpleasant process of having additional eggs extracted; a supply of defrosted embryos is available for implantation at any future time.

From one point of view, this all seems like a sensible and wonderful way of enabling otherwise infertile couples to have a family. From another, it begins to take on the flavor of the brave new world. Embryos are already being selected, and then implanted or discarded (i.e., killed), on the basis of their genetic qualities. The motive here has, of course, been to get rid of some genetic diseases by getting rid of the embryonic human beings afflicted by those diseases. Already we have examples of "pre-implantation genetic diagnosis" (PGD) being used to provide transplant donors for older children.

The principles and the mechanisms are in place to enable any human birth to be screened and any human being to be selected for quality. Quality control of human beings has arrived.

We have already mentioned the movie *Gattaca*. In the story, a family has two sons. They decide, against the trend, to have their first child without using the in vitro techniques that have become standard in their world. They opt for what is known as a "faith birth" or a "God-child." So immediately after Vincent's birth he is tested and his parents given the predictions for his life on the basis of what is known about his genes. He has a high chance of early death from heart disease, as well as other ailments. Much of the movie focuses on the discrimination against Vincent, both in the home (despite his parents' evident love for him), in school (a kindergarten refuses to admit him as school insurance will not permit it), and work (despite laws that forbid "genoism" – genetic discrimination).

When they decide to have a second child, they abandon "faith births" and join the crowd. Once bitten, twice shy. Their embryos are screened and they are given sophisticated choices. What do they want to screen out, and – despite their initial reluctance – what do they want to add? What can they afford? "He will still be you," says the helpful MD, "just the very best of you."

While some of the options still lie beyond what science can achieve, the in vitro technology is the same we have been using for nearly thirty years. The principle of pre-implantation genetic diagnosis has been established, and also, as we have seen, the principle of using it for more than screening out serious illnesses. What we do with it is up to us; the mechanism is already in place.

The second problem involves the extra embryos. It amazes us that so many people have decided to make embryos and then deep-freeze the children God has given them, their flesh and blood, members of their families – as if they were retirement savings in the bank or left-overs from Sunday lunch. Some people now use the term "Popsicles" to describe these frozen embryo children. That trivializing word shows how far we have already come toward turning our children into commodities.

If you aren't pro-life, freezing embryos may seem to make good sense. If life does not begin in any morally important sense until some later stage, making extra embryos and freezing them in case they are ever wanted seems convenient, minimizes cost, and cuts down unpleasant treatment for the woman involved. "Popsicles" make sense for people who think like that.

But how can "Popsicles" make sense to people like us who believe that every human life begins at conception/fertilization, and that these tiny deep-frozen human beings therefore bear the image of God?

Some have pointed out that a surprisingly high number of naturally conceived embryos don't make it to live birth and often die before they implant. That may seem like an appealing argument in favor of not taking embryos very seriously, as if the fact that many of them die in

Pope John Paul II on In Vitro

The various techniques of artificial reproduction, which would seem to be at the service of life and which are frequently used with this intention, actually open the door to new threats against life. Apart from the fact that they are morally unacceptable, since they separate procreation from the fully human context of the conjugal act, these techniques have a high rate of failure: not just failure in relation to fertilization but with regard to the subsequent development of the embryo, which is exposed to the risk of death, generally within a very short space of time. Furthermore, the number of embryos produced is often greater than that needed for implantation in the woman's womb, and these so-called "spare embryos" are then destroyed or used for research which, under the pretext of scientific or medical progress, in fact reduces human life to the level of simple "biological material" to be freely disposed of.

the womb frees us to take risks with them. Yet once you think about it, such an argument loses much of its appeal.

What about the high rates of babies and young children who die through famine and disease in primitive parts of the world? Does that make them less valuable? As we know too well, one day we shall all die. Christians know something about why we die (ultimately, because of sin), and the hope we have (of the resurrection). As George Bernard Shaw once said, the "ultimate statistic" is that "one out of one dies." Some die very, very young; some in advanced age. Yet all are precious, made in the image of God. And all are 100 percent human!

WEIRDER SCENARIOS

Plenty of other options exist. The in vitro technique allows for endless flexibility.

John and Sue may decide to have a child and to use in vitro because they have problems conceiving naturally, using their "own" genetic material, his sperm and her egg. Or they may decide to use one or other or both gamete(s) from "donors," either friends or someone

The Egg Trade

Several years ago I took part in a PBS *Frontline* television program that examined in vitro and the ways it was being used. The program focused on a lesbian couple and their plan to use in vitro to have children – taking it in turns and searching for sperm donors on the Internet. It is not difficult to find well-qualified donors for sperm, all the way up to Nobel prize winners and sports stars.

Buying eggs is more complicated, since it is much more difficult for women to "donate" them. Campus newspapers around the country now regularly carry ads seeking coeds as donors and offering five to ten thousand dollars and more – up to $100,000, apparently, for tall, attractive, high-intelligence women at Ivy League schools. Colleges have begun to place notices about egg donation on student employment bulletin boards.

NIGEL CAMERON

found through Internet searches and the placing of ads. In either case, they may decide to ask another woman, a surrogate, to be the womb-provider for their child so that Sue does not have to give up her high-paying job (or if she does not want to face the demands of carrying the child).

Part of our problem lies in the fact that those who made the case for this technology back in the 1970s and 1980s were not arguing for quality control, or "spare" embryos for research or freezing. They did not make a case for splitting parenting into three so that busy people with money and/or not-so-good genes could have brilliant children with minimum interruption to their lifestyles. That would not have gained much public sympathy! The infertility case may have been presented as a "good" one, yet the technology has let loose its own values and is placing wholly new pressures, for example, on single Christian women who wish they had babies but who have no more interest in marriage than they have in casual sex. And the scene is set for more sophisticated temptations: for increasingly detailed quality control before implantation; for couples to get "better" babies by using other people's gametes; for busy lifestyles to lead to more use of surrogacy.

A Memorable Phone Call

I shall never forget the call. It came one morning during term and while I briefly visited my office between classes at Trinity Evangelical Divinity School. The call came from an elder at a big evangelical church, who said it was urgent. So I listened.

He needed advice about a woman in the church. She was fortyish, a member of the choir, pregnant, and had been told she had to stay in the hospital for the rest of the pregnancy because of pre-eclampsia (high blood pressure). Should the deacons' fund help with her medical costs?

I waited because I felt sure there had to be more to the story; there was. He had been visiting patients in the hospital and had learned she was in his church, so he had stopped by her room. He introduced himself and said he did not think he knew her husband. "Oh, I'm not married," she quickly answered. He felt embarrassed and made a comment like, "I'm sorry; I suppose accidents happen."

"This wasn't an accident!" she replied indignantly. "And I wouldn't dream of sleeping with a man outside marriage. This is a test-tube baby."

Still the story went on. This single woman had gone to a pastor for counsel. She desired to have a baby. She did not know anyone she wanted to marry. She certainly would not have sex with someone outside marriage. And so *the pastor* suggested to her that in vitro fertilization offered the answer to her problems. No need for marriage, no need for sex; a nice, clean, clinical way of making babies.

I told the elder that I thought they should help with her costs (her insurance had run out), not least as the church might be legally liable, since it had advised her to get pregnant that way.

It gets worse. A year later I taught a grad class in bioethics. One evening's lecture focused on the ethics of in vitro fertilization. I used the story of the church elder and the choir member to help make my point. Afterwards a grad student, single, in her thirties, took me aside to tell me how unfeeling I was to discuss the subject like that. She has more than one friend, she told me, who had considered in vitro for just the same reason—to have a baby without getting married or having to have sex outside marriage. How could I say that was wrong?

Nigel Cameron

"Our children are creations, not commodities," said President Bush. It's clear that the difference is becoming blurred.

WHY IT MATTERS SO MUCH

In vitro has been around for a generation, and screening techniques that already enable us to pick positive characteristics in our babies are getting more sophisticated every day. And we are getting used to these ways of thinking. So when we move further up the steep curve of discovery and commercialization, it is going to be ever more difficult to say "No!"

When tomorrow's technologies come on line, we need to be ready, and we have so much ground to make up. The other side—the people who don't care, who will profit, or who positively favor reshaping our human nature—already are in place.

Already they use the phrase "taking control of our own evolution." They use terms like "transhumanism" and "posthumanism." A blue baby? A baby with wings? *You* choose. All of a sudden, we have in our hands technology that makes *us* the subject of our experiments and remodeling.

That's what C. S. Lewis meant by his prophetic phrase "the abolition of man." We shall have in our power the technology to abolish "man" as we have known the human species, and turn ourselves into something else.

Every mother wants the best for her baby. Every mother dreams of her child having every chance for health and happiness. And so, she prays and plans the way for that little one.

Kate is one such mother. Her first three children had been healthy, and she felt sure her next baby would be too. She didn't want to have the amniocentesis procedure in order to avoid even the slightest risk that the insertion of the needle into her uterus would cause her to miscarry. When doctors told her there was a new way to assess the chance of abnormalities with no risk of miscarriage—a blood test and a special sonogram—Kate happily made the appointment.

The results signaled that her unborn child had a high chance of having Down syndrome. Suddenly, Kate was catapulted into a growing group of prospective parents who must wrestle with end-of-life decisions before their child takes his first breath.

Who would have thought a decade ago that a simple blood test could reveal so much? Who would have imagined that the resolution on sonograms would become so detailed that the smallest of abnormalities could be detected? Today, high-resolution sonograms can detect everything from brain cysts to a cleft palate. Most couples appreciate having the new information ... but the choices it foists on them force them to carry tremendous burdens.

A choice such as Kate and her husband face.

What defect gives reason enough to end a pregnancy that had been very much wanted? Some defects could be partly treated, but doctors and genetic counselors often leave couples alone for the hard conversations about abortion or how having a child with a disability would affect the family. Kate and her husband wrestled over what to do. Finally, she ended her pregnancy. "It was the hardest decision I ever had to make," she said.

I wonder what made Kate decide to abort her unborn child with Down syndrome? Did she think he would find no happiness in life? Or did she worry about the burden this young life would place on her family? Was it motivated by a fear of financial strain? Even some doctors who perform abortions feel uncomfortable as some women choose to quietly abort fetuses with relatively minor defects.

As a person with a serious disability, this all makes me *very* nervous. I see a grass-roots eugenics movement beginning to evolve that ultimately will lead to a greater intolerance of disabilities. Our society has a fundamental fear of disability, and we are letting that fear drive everything from laws and policies to the quiet hints in ob-gyn offices that an unborn child is "better off dead than disabled."

I wish people would see that a disability can provide the passport into a richer life and a deeper happiness than Kate would ever dream for her child. James 1:2–5 says, "Consider it pure joy, my brothers, whenever you face trials of many kinds, because you know that the testing of your faith develops perseverance. Perseverance must finish its work so that you may be mature and complete, not lacking anything."

True, a disability is hard—but it can also powerfully unite a family. It can refine a family's character and set of values. It can force one to see the joy in simple achievements and pleasures. A disability can foster faith, a deeper prayer life, and a respect for God and his Word. Most of all, it can force us into the arms of the Lord of grace: "But this happened that we might not rely on ourselves but on God, who raises the dead" (2 Corinthians 1:9). And that's a good thing. A very good thing.

Our fixation on perfection is eating away at the human soul. A better fixation might be 2 Corinthians 4:18, "So we fix our eyes not on what is seen, but on what is unseen. For what is seen is temporary, but what is unseen is eternal." Like me with quadriplegia, it's something people with Down syndrome do every day.

JONI

PART THREE

Treating People Like Things

The biggest political issue of the opening years of the twenty-first century has been "therapeutic cloning." That's the term some scientists have made up for cloning human embryos in huge numbers so they can be used for research and to produce medications. The practice has horrified even pro-choice advocates.

Meanwhile, genetic discrimination is on the march — the idea that how you are treated in society should depend on the kind of genes you have. Already insurance companies and employers have discovered genetic information and used it to undermine your rights and your dignity.

Did you know that the biotech industry wants to be able to own human beings? Already it has patented genes; now it wants to be able to patent embryos and fetuses.

Side by side with advances in biology, other technologies are starting to threaten human dignity. This still seems like science fiction, but some people are getting very serious about it — using computers to "enhance" human beings and finally, perhaps, to replace us.

All these topics have one thing in common: they break down the barrier between people and things.

HUMAN HARVEST

Our society has a fundamental fear of suffering. We hate it. Our culture has utter disdain for it. We want to eradicate it, ignore it, "shut it up" with ibuprofen, surgically exorcise it, divorce, escape, kill, clone, or cure it. *Anything* but deal with it. We have nothing but contempt for suffering, for anything that makes life hard or unpleasant.

When it comes to treating people like things, it's only a short philosophical hop, skip, and a jump to where contempt extends to *people* who suffer: people who strain Medicare or drain the grandkids' college fund ... people who produce nothing and contribute nothing more to society than bills and increased medical costs ... people — like preborn or even newborn infants with disabilities — who might encroach on a family's economic security and who seem to have no real potential for a good quality of life. If our culture can't fix it, cure it, medicate it, sedate it, or surgically remove it, then please get rid of it — because we sure can't live with it.

In a society with no tools, no true moral guidelines for dealing with pain and affliction, discomfort or inconvenience, the people deemed dispensable are the ones who ultimately suffer. People like the weak and infirm, the elderly and senile, the embryo and the infant. When we have no moral and spiritual resources to shape our view of affliction, then society slips into its "natural selection" way of looking at suffering; and it is the medically fragile who feel the brunt.

It opens the way to "treating people like things."

It's why I got involved in the case of Terri Schiavo. Terri was the severely brain-injured Florida woman whose estranged husband fought through the courts to have her feeding tube removed. He maintained that "Terri wouldn't want to live this way." Never mind that Mr. Schiavo was living with another woman and had fathered two of her children. Some in our society say that he should be allowed to "get on with his life." Some believe he actually demonstrated compassion toward his disabled wife.

Those of us with disabilities see it differently. We believe he was blinded by contempt – not only for Terri, but for millions of Americans with disabilities whose lives came in jeopardy the moment the courts ruled in his favor.

If we strip away the heart-wrenching emotions surrounding the case of Terri Schiavo, we are left with a single question: What life value does a person have who cannot speak, move, hear, or see? What standard of evidence should we require when determining the healthcare wishes of a person unable to speak for himself? The Florida courts ruled that Terri's husband's recollection of her casual comment after a television program will suffice. Talk about contempt! The courts disguise their prejudice against "disability" with the cloak of "Terri's right to privacy," but the fact remains, they ignored her right to life, her right to humane treatment, and her right to rehabilitative therapy. They held her in contempt because of her suffering.

As a quadriplegic, I'm appalled that national polls seemed to favor Mr. Schiavo and the Florida courts. Our society's disdain of suffering has now, indeed, extended to *those who suffer*, those who are severely brain-damaged, minimally conscious, in comas or persistent vegetative states. They are in deep trouble. They are on the verge of being treated as *things*.

God help us.

JONI

For several months before 9/11, the dominant issue in American politics was not the economy or national security, but whether the US should fund research on human embryos. It was so important that President Bush chose to make it the topic of his first televised broadcast to the nation. Commentators suggested that this could be the "defining issue" of the Bush presidency. Those of us who had been saying for years that the questions raised by biotechnology would dominate the twenty-first century saw our predictions starting to come true.

And while the terrorist attacks and the US response soon drowned the biotech discussion, it returned in full force in the 2004 election campaign. The highlight of the Democratic Convention was a speech by Ron Reagan Jr., son of the late president, that praised the possibilities of what is known as "therapeutic cloning" (though he avoided using the phrase). Senator John Edwards, Democratic candidate for vice president, declared in one of the most bizarre statements in American politics that with Senator John Kerry, the Democratic challenger, as president, people like quadriplegic superstar Christopher Reeve would be able to walk again. The "biotech century" had arrived!

We saw in chapter 6 how cloning works. An embryo is created without the need for sperm to fertilize an egg. Instead, scientists replace the genetic material in the egg with some from another cell – in principle, from any nonreproductive cell. Embryo research itself is not new. It has been possible since the 1970s, when in vitro fertilization was developed. But in the past, most scientists and governments have remained wary of the ethics of experimenting on embryos, especially if it involved creating them specially for that purpose. The UK, where both in vitro and cloning were first invented, has long been the most liberal nation in the Western world in its approach to these technologies and human dignity. In the US, some states have laws that forbid embryo research. While no federal law exists on the issue, no administration, Democratic or Republican, has ever funded research that destroys embryos.

But cloning has changed the climate among scientists and also in the press. Its dehumanized method of making humans, since it does not involve the penetration of an egg by a sperm, makes it even more offensive to some people, so deep distaste toward experimental cloning began to take hold early in the debate. It looked very likely that Congress would vote to outlaw the technology, as have many other nations.

But things changed. Enthusiasm began to grow in the scientific and biotech communities for so-called "therapeutic" cloning as a possible treatment for incurable diseases, such as Alzheimer's and Parkinson's, through the mass production of embryonic stem cells tailored to the patient. And the biotech industry, through its Washington-based trade organization BIO (the Biotechnology Industry Organization), stepped up its advocacy using vast resources that included radio and print ads, lobbying, and donations to Republican groups as well as other political funds. They pressed the possibility of curing these and other diseases, if only they could manufacture cloned embryos for experiments and to produce one-on-one medications.

They used many techniques to make their point and focus media attention on the need for "Cures Now," to quote the name of one of their organizations. They paraded celebrities before congressional committees and the media (most memorably Christopher Reeve in his wheelchair), and among other stunts staged a gruesome "hanging" of handicapped people to illustrate how those who opposed cloning were sentencing them to death.

On the other side of the fence, three things were in progress. First, Christians continued to get organized. Though without the vast resources available to the biotech industry, a combination of pro-life and pro-family groups, together with the Southern Baptist Christian Life Commission and the US Conference of Catholic Bishops, worked closely in cooperation to inform their diverse constituencies of the importance of these issues, and to encourage them to pressure their representatives on Capitol Hill. Second, an informal coalition brought together pro-life leaders and representatives of environmentalist and pro-choice feminist groups, together with others, including some (pro-choice) United Methodists – pro-choice groups that on this issue allied with pro-lifers, and sought either a ban on all cloning, or at least a serious moratorium. Third, the science debate took some unlikely turns. It became increasingly clear that the claims for "therapeutic" cloning using tailor-made clonal embryos to manufacture medicine were mainly hype. Meanwhile, every few days an article would appear showing that "adult" stem cells could do the job better – and in many cases, *now*.

How Do We Ban Cloning?

Two basic approaches have been proposed for how to ban cloning, both in the US and around the world. One favors a partial ban with the goal of preventing the birth of cloned babies; it permits the cloning of human embryos for research. The second approach is comprehensive, prohibiting any use of cloning technology involving the human species.

At first sight, the partial-ban approach seems prudent. It gains support from two very different groups: those who favor a comprehensive cloning ban but who wish to attain it in two stages; and those who wish to ban the birth of cloned babies but who support the cloning of human embryos for research. But this approach has some clear problems.

First, if the cloning of embryos for research is permitted, the policy can be applied only by requiring that they also be destroyed. Since biotech advocates need very large numbers of embryos for the "therapeutic cloning" model to work, very large numbers of embryos must be destroyed. Policy makers with varied views on the nature of early embryonic human life have found the principle of creating and destroying huge numbers of embryonic human beings unacceptable.

Second, if the cloning of embryos for research is permitted, it will perfect the very technology that can be used to clone embryos for implantation and live birth.

Third, if the cloning of embryos for research is permitted, many millions of cloned human embryos will be produced in laboratories. It is inevitable that some of these embryos will be implanted and result in the birth of cloned babies. Many motives will be cited, all the way from criminal intent and financial reward to pro-life "rescue." One way or another, the mass production of research-cloned embryos will result in the birth of cloned children.

In fact, there is no better way to protect against the mass production of human embryos for experimental purposes than by putting in place a "cloning ban." Encouraging the mass production of embryos will make more, not less, likely the birth of cloned human beings.

Amazing Stem Cells

Much of the debate has turned on "stem cells," those cells that have the inbuilt capacity to become other cells. That means that, in principle, they could cure diseases in which cells are damaged, diseases—like

Parkinson's and Alzheimer's—that are devastating and have proved hard to treat. Stem cells in the embryo can be used only by destroying the embryo (at four or five days old). Stem cells also exist in the blood from the umbilical cord, and in many parts of the adult body. Big debates are taking place about which of these many stem cells will prove the most useful in curing terrible diseases. But, so far, all the cures are coming from "adult" stem cells that do not involve destroying embryos.

Unfortunately, the media has chosen to focus on the unproved promise of embryo stem cells and almost entirely ignores the real cures already demonstrated from "adult" cells. Dr. James Dobson, founder of Focus on the Family, spoke to journalists at the National Press Club, pleading with them for honest reporting. "Embryonic stem cells are not going to be the source of a cure for Alzheimer's," he declared. He continued: "Are you aware that not one human being anywhere in the world is being treated with embryonic stem cells? There is not a single clinical trial going on anywhere in the world, because embryonic stem cells in laboratory animals ... create tumors. Nobody will use them."

The term "therapeutic cloning" has been coined to describe a powerful idea. Many scientists want to be able to clone you and me, so that stem cells may be harvested from our own twin embryos and used to treat our diseases. This is the idea that Ron Reagan Jr. promoted at the Democratic Convention in 2004. No one knows if this will work; it has not been done reliably even on animals. And it involves what many of us see as the ultimate horror: you clone yourself so that your own twin brother or sister, destroyed as an embryo, provides medication to cure you. Make no mistake: This is a human harvest.

CLONING ON THE COASTS: NEW JERSEY AND CALIFORNIA

But it gets worse. In the state of New Jersey, a bill signed into law in January of 2004 not only permitted cloning to make embryos to produce stem cells, but permitted the implantation of the cloned embryo in the womb—so long as there is no live-born baby. What did its sponsors have in mind?

Representatives of the biotech industry pushed for the bill. There is only one reason they could have included this provision: They intend, down the line, to solve the problem of generating new tissue by implanting the cloned embryo in a uterus, growing the embryo for weeks until organs and other tissues develop, and then using those tissues for transplant. This gruesome future takes the idea of a "human harvest" further into the brave new world. It is the only logical explanation for the way the New Jersey law was written.

Meanwhile, in California, a combination of celebrities and investors spent some $35 million to set up an institute for stem cell research through Proposition 71, an amendment to the state constitution. The initiative was passed by a 59–41 percent margin in November 2004, fed by expensive and dishonest TV advertising (they outspent opponents of the measure by around 100:1). The institute has $3 billion of funding and will focus on embryo stem cell research—and cloning to get the embryos. This bizarre project already has produced startling effects in other states, as they rush to fund their own projects. No one is asking (a) whether it will ever work (there is almost no private investment going into embryo stem cell research, which suggests that savvy biotech investors are taking a pass); or (b) why countries like Canada have decided to ban it.

As Steve Milloy, publisher of JunkScience.com, commented on Fox News: "If embryonic stem cell research had real and imminent possibilities, private investors would be pouring capital into research, hoping for real and imminent profits. Instead, venture capital firms are contributing to political efforts to get taxpayers to fund research.... What the venture capitalists seem to be hoping for is that taxpayer funding of stem cell research will increase the value of their stakes in biotech companies. The venture capitalists can then cash out at a hefty profit, leaving taxpayers holding the bag of fruitless research."

THE GLOBAL DEBATE

To underline the unique significance of this debate, the United Nations has discussed proposals to develop an international convention that would ban cloning around the world.

Rebecca Griffin's Story

"Alzheimer's disease" was a familiar term to me long before it became the hot topic on the Hill because of President Reagan.... I was only nine years old when my father was diagnosed with Alzheimer's disease, and I spent the next seven years as one of his primary caregivers, along with my mother. We cared for him at home because we couldn't afford to put him in a nursing home until the beginning of my senior year of high school. He died two weeks before finals my freshman year of college. I hadn't seen him since Christmas.

The events surrounding Reagan's death struck a very personal note for me, but the policy debates that will intensify because of them will likely hit even closer to home.

"Embryonic stem cell research" is almost always mentioned in the same breath as Alzheimer's disease, floated as the way to reach the cure, or at least ease the suffering. This seemingly worthy cause gets many celebrity endorsements, from Nancy Reagan to Michael J. Fox and Christopher Reeve, all with their own twists on the miracles it could create....

As a caregiver who has lived through the situation myself, who has heard all the sweet promises handed out after the hopeless diagnosis, I say this to other sufferers: don't listen to them. Don't buy into this hoax.

The appeal to caregivers is the attractant on a moral Venus flytrap. Those who push for a lifting of the experimental ban and for government funding of the research dangle hope in front of desperate, hurting people, in return for public support. It is exploitation at its most debased and repugnant, but too many are letting themselves be persuaded anyway.

But even if there's no hope for us, what about the people who will be diagnosed in the future? That's an equally powerful line of argument; we all fear getting older, and especially those of us who have been caregivers are terrified of what might happen to us. Medical science has advanced by leaps and bounds just over the past couple of decades without this macabre research. Besides, if we open this door, where do we stop? We set ourselves up as the ones who get to decide who has the right to live, and who doesn't, who has a disease that's important enough to cure, and who needs to just suffer – who is really a human being, and who isn't. If you're created in a petri dish, you're not a human; if you're created in a womb, you are: what kind of brave new world do we want to pass on to our descendants, assuming we even have any?

I have another perspective on the embryonic stem cell debate – because of my father's age, I had to be conceived in vitro by a sperm donor. I was one of those "test tube babies" that could just as easily have been sacrificed because I wasn't quite human enough to matter.

Germany and France first came to the United Nations in 2001 with a proposal for a ban on "reproductive cloning" – that is, cloning that produces a live-born baby. They apparently expected swift agreement to their proposal and were surprised to find firm opposition from the United States. The US took the view that only a comprehensive ban on cloning would achieve the desired result – to prevent the birth of cloned babies. A halfway house that permitted the development of cloning for embryo research would in the end make it more likely that cloned babies would be born. In the spring of 2005, the United Nations General Assembly voted by nearly 3-1 in favor of the United Nations Declaration on Human Cloning, calling on all nations to prohibit all forms of human cloning.

Meanwhile, the world's first bioethics treaty, the European Convention on Biomedicine and Human Rights, has been signed by many European states. Article 18 of the treaty prohibits the creation of embryos for research. An extra "protocol" has been added that bans human cloning, although without specifying how cloning should be prohibited and – as diplomats sometimes do – using ambiguity to cover up disagreement. If the cloning ban and the ban on creating embryos for research are put together, however, the world's one bioethics treaty plainly bans embryo cloning for *any* purpose.

This reflects the position of many European countries. Americans often speak of Europe as "liberal" and "post-Christian," and to a degree they are right. Church attendance is far lower than in the US, and there are much smaller pro-life movements in Europe. But on these biotech questions, very conservative positions have been taken in many countries, beginning with Germany, which since World War II has served as the conscience of the world on biotechnology. As we saw in chapter 4, Germany knows from its Nazi past what it means to have science and scientists run out of ethical control, and so German science is marked by a determination that it will never happen again.

Germany banned cloning (for any purpose) back in 1990; many other countries followed suit, including, most recently, Canada and France. Other countries with comprehensive cloning bans include Australia and Norway. Many nations – including those with liberal abortion laws and small pro-life movements – have decided to prohibit "therapeutic cloning."

The world needs to follow their lead.

Every night my paralysis forces me to bed around 8:00 p.m. It's partly because my body is wearing out after more than thirty-eight years in a wheelchair. In bed, I look face up at the ceiling and let gravity sink me into my mattress. It's a good time to pray; it's also a chance to watch some good TV. Last night I flicked on a PBS special, "Innovation: Miracle Cell." When I learned it described the new therapies under development using adult stem cells, I asked my husband to turn up the volume.

The program immediately gripped me. The camera focused on nineteen-year-old Laura Dominguez, sitting in her wheelchair. Laura broke her neck and became paralyzed after a car accident in 2001. She smiled, looking young, bright, and attractive. She had reason to smile. Last year, Laura traveled to Portugal for an extraordinary operation. First, they drew stem cells — her body's own "repair cells" — from the lining in her nose, delicately separating the cells and treating them with awe and respect. So they should; those cells were like blank slates, able to turn into most any tissue, including that which would "fit" in Laura's spinal cord. The doctors then transplanted the miracle cells, gently packing them into the damaged portion of her spine. Three months later, Laura could move her foot and regained a significant amount of feeling in her back and legs.

For me, a quadriplegic, the amazing news took my breath away.

One doctor smiled at the interviewer and stated, "I will be able to say to somebody with a spinal cord injury, 'Yes, you will walk again,'

Miracle Cells

My daughter is Laura Dominguez, who is one of the first Americans to have adult stem cell surgery in Portugal by Dr. Carlos Lima. It has been brought to my attention that you have mentioned my daughter's name when talking about adult stem cells. My daughter, in our opinion, is living poof that the Portugal procedure works and that adult stem cells are miracle cells.

— ABEL DOMINGUEZ IN A PERSONAL EMAIL
TO JONI EARECKSON TADA, FEBRUARY 8, 2005

as opposed to telling them, 'Life is good from a wheelchair.'" I smiled too and thought of the irony of doing so—there I was, a chronic spinal-cord-injured woman, lying paralyzed in bed, rejoicing in the success of another's healing.

The TV program highlighted other success stories: a teenager with a punctured heart, healed through a stem cell transplant from his own blood; a little boy who no longer has cancer because of a transplant using stem cells from the umbilical cord of his little brother; and more spinal-cord-injured persons who are seeing amazing progress from transplants using stem cells from their own bone marrow and nose tissue.

It thrilled me to think of the many paralyzed people who, as I write, are applying for similar new therapies here in the US. About one hundred people in wheelchairs soon will have the chance to undergo the same operation. No wonder they are excited! Adult stem cell transplants are safe, with no chance of tissue rejection—and for the most part, they're successful. These incredible new therapies are giving hope to people and helping them regain functional skills and some movement!

The thing that struck me most was the doctors' comments. One doctor announced that, "Self-therapy is *safe* therapy!" Another said, "This will revolutionize modern medicine!" Another doctor applauded how *natural*, how relatively easy regenerative medicine is. Stem cells from embryos are programmed to grow; stem cells from adults are there to heal and restore. *That's* what encouraged me most as I lay in bed. Yes, I am a quadriplegic and aware of the need for spinal cord injury cure; but I'm also a Christian concerned that a cure be both safe *and* ethical.

Ethical Stem Cells Work!

Hwang Mi-soon had been paralyzed and bedridden for 19 years due to a back injury. About 30 days after the [adult stem cell] operation, Hwang stood up from her wheelchair and shuffled a few paces back and forth with the help of a walking frame. With tears in her eyes, she said at last week's press conference, "This is already a miracle for me. I never dreamed of getting on my feet again."

Korea Times

I watched young Laura Dominguez lift her leg and beam with joy. Whether regenerative medicine is for me, is not the issue. The point is this: *There is hope.* Real, amazing, within-reach *hope!* Hope for people with spinal cord injuries, with heart disease, diabetes, Alzheimer's, and cancer.

But some people refuse hope.

Michael Kinsley works as an editor at the *Los Angeles Times.* He's also been struggling with Parkinson's disease since 1993. He is looking for a cure. Fast. He's frustrated that President Bush has upheld a ban on using taxpayer money to fund the destruction of human embryos in order to harvest their stem cells. (Never mind that Bush's administration was the first to come up with a compromise permitting federal funds to go toward research on a limited number of private stem cell lines.) Michael still reasons, "Meanwhile, there are nearly 400,000 human embryos sitting in the freezers of fertility clinics, almost all of which will eventually be destroyed."

The reasoning is flat and pragmatic. If you believe that destroying an embryo is not on the same moral plane as murdering your neighbor, then what's the fuss? Michael says, "Anyone who opposes stem cell research on moral grounds had better be willing to look me in the eye and say: 'Mike, I know that preventing stem cell research means blocking a major avenue of hope for you and one million American Parkinson's sufferers, as well as for victims of other diseases, including cancer. I know that an embryo is a clump of cells invisible to the naked eye ... but I would rather ruin your life, health, and hopes than allow this miracle research to continue.' "

Well, I was willing to look Michael Kinsley "in the eye" when we debated this subject on PAX TV's "Faith under Fire." With my spinal cord injury, and his Parkinson's, we appeared to be on a level playing field. That's about all we had in common. Mr. Kinsley insisted that an embryo is on the same plane as a potato. Worthless. To be used or discarded.

During the debate, I reminded him that he began his journey on planet Earth as one of those embryos. It didn't seem to faze him. Neither did the examples I listed of paralyzed people who are now walking as a result of adult stem cell therapies. What's more, Mr. Kinsley refused to hear about the advancements already happening in treating Parkinson's with adult tissue therapies. Like so many in politics and the media who seem enamored by the pharmaceutical companies, venture capitalists, and biotech industry, Mr. Kinsley would rather remain morbidly fixated on a lie (like Gollum in *The Lord of the Rings*) than seek honest-to-goodness hope and healing. As we debated I felt sad for him.

I'm not the one ruining Michael Kinsley's health and hopes. Just like that sad little creature in *The Lord of the Rings*, his injury is self-inflicted. For there *is* hope. There *are* answers. There *is* life and health. All he needs to do is walk into the Detroit Medical Center sometime to watch Laura Dominguez practice walking with her braces.

JONI

CHAPTER 9

THE COLOR OF YOUR GENES

"Joni, in the last twenty years, we have seen technological development *double*—double since the Iron Age!"

My friend, a graduate from MIT, knew what he was talking about.

"What's more, it'll double again in the next few years." *That*, I knew. One year ago I purchased a new computer with 28.6 gigabytes of storage and enough power to run a spread sheet, send email, do word processing, navigate the Internet, and look up Bible texts, all at the same time, using my voice activation dictating program. That was a year ago. Yesterday when I got my voice activation upgrade, I was told I needed a new computer with more power, speed, and memory. (It's a good thing prices keep coming down.)

What an amazing world we live in! I wish the prophet Daniel could have lived to see this day. Then again, maybe he did. Perhaps he saw CNN in some prophetic vision and could only watch in wide-eyed wonder at all the technological advancements. Maybe his brain could absorb only so much and he turned away just in time to hear God say, "But thou, O Daniel, shut up the words, and seal the book, even to the time of the end: many shall run to and fro, and knowledge shall be increased" (Daniel 12:4 KJV).

Knowledge is flying at us from right and left. We grasp something new (or purchase a computer) only to find it obsolete a few months later. Do the proliferation of knowledge and the jet-blast speed of technological changes mean we are close to the time of the end?

I don't know, but it makes me look at the time when human knowledge was barely budding. Genesis 2:9 says, "The LORD God made all kinds of trees grow out of the ground—trees that were pleasing to the eye and good for food. In the middle of the garden were the tree of life and the tree of the knowledge of good and evil." We all know what happened next. A piece of fruit got plucked from the tree of the knowledge of good and evil, stripping away man's innocence, and he was left bearing the responsibilities of knowledge. Knowledge of what was good *and* evil.

Little wonder God wasted no time in taking action. In Genesis chapter 3, "The LORD God said, 'The man has now become like one of us, knowing good and evil. He must not be allowed to reach out his hand and take also from the tree of life and eat, and live forever.' So the LORD God banished him from the Garden of Eden to work the ground from which he had been taken. After he drove the man out, he placed on the east side of the Garden of Eden cherubim and a flaming sword flashing back and forth to guard the way to the tree of life" (v. 22 – 24).

Some people think God was unkind in banishing Adam and Eve from the garden. Some see the cherubim with the flaming sword as adding insult to injury. *Why would God make such a big deal about the tree of life?*

How merciful of God to keep sin-sick man from eating of the tree of life! Had Adam and Eve been able to make their way back into the garden, mankind in his sad and sorry state would have lived forever. Who wants to live in a body of sin and death? Not me.

From the first time the word *knowledge* is used in the Bible, it clearly carries a sobering responsibility. It is a double-edged sword. Knowledge has two sides: good ... and evil. It's been that way since before the Iron Age. And it remains true today.

"The tree of the knowledge of good and evil" has a direct bearing on all that we've covered in this book. Because for every technical advancement for good, there is always an accompanying potential for evil — in everything from splitting atoms to the color of your genes.

What of the future? Daniel the prophet declares to us that at "the time of the end: many shall run to and fro, and knowledge shall be increased." My computer guy will tell you that knowledge is increasing at breakneck speed. This is good ... and not so good. As scientific knowledge continues to grow, we need Christians who will go before us and help lay the framework for prudent decision making. When it comes to grappling with the essence of all that it means to be human, when it comes to manipulating the tiniest of genes on a thread of DNA, let's

remember we are touching a very peculiar fruit; not an apple hanging on a tree in a garden ...

... but the apple of God's eye.

JONI

Now that eugenic abortion has become routine, along with the eugenic screening of in vitro embryos, it is no surprise that the eugenic pressures are mounting for humans in later stages in life.

Eugenics has two sides. People with weak genes find themselves at a further disadvantage, while people with strong genes get special privileges. The aim is to discourage some and encourage the others.

Abortion has made eugenic killing widespread and legal in many countries. To be fair to some pro-choice feminists, the more conscientious people who favor abortion as a woman's right are often alarmed by its use to destroy the handicapped and genetically "inferior." The pressure is on to take the lives of "inferior" babies who make it through pregnancy to birth early in life. Princeton's infamous bioethics professor, Peter Singer, has argued that parents should have the right to take the life of a born handicapped infant.

On the other hand, eugenics seeks to encourage people with "good" genes. The growing market for eggs and sperm from "superior" women and men shows one way this eugenic initiative is moving forward.

Meanwhile, what about those who are already born, who have not been killed and who have genetic problems? In fact, we all have genetic abnormalities of one kind or another; but what about those for whom they could be serious? Who should know, and what should they be able to do with what they know?

A Great Movie

We have already talked about *Gattaca*. Like Mary Shelley's novel *Frankenstein* from two centuries ago, and Aldous Huxley's *Brave New World*, it's a masterpiece that tells a story about the future so that we look at things in the present in a very different way. We already have some of the technology featured in the movie; some is not too far off. It catches our attention in part by a retro feel that mingles with the futurist aspects of the story—the use of sepia tones and cars that look old-fashioned even as they run on electricity.

Its theme tackles the biggest question we face today: what do we do with our newfound knowledge of genetics? Should we employ it to design and "perfect" our children? Do we want to know, as a baby is born, the diseases he or she likely will suffer from, and how long the individual is likely to live? Should we be free to find out the most intimate genetic secrets of anyone we wish? What should employers do with this information?

These are vital questions, and they are for today, not tomorrow. Even now, several bills on Capitol Hill seek to outlaw "genetic discrimination." President Bush has made speeches against it. But coupled with the push for a new eugenics to give us "designer babies" and a focus on screening out diseased or "inferior" embryos and fetuses, its implications are not easy.

Gattaca raises the key questions. Should we assign those whom we know to have weak or defective genes to menial tasks? Should we give those with "good" genes the big breaks? It may sound reasonable enough. But, if it does, we have begun to buy into eugenics. Eugenics always *sounds* reasonable ... at first. Perhaps the most profound theme of *Gattaca* is that people with "superior genes" also suffer in this eugenic world, and perhaps suffer more than those who are genetically weak and of whom expectations are correspondingly low (and for whom the movie coins two telling terms: the "in-valid," and the "de-gene-erate").

The DVD version features extra scenes, deleted from the original, and right at the end we get a compelling series of frames (that we won't spoil by describing for you). But you will note, right at the start, a quote from the Old Testament. And while the movie is devoid of religion (it was not made by or for believers), and none of the characters is presented as a model of Christian living, the power of the narrative—as in those two great books by Mary Shelley and Aldous Huxley—is unforgettable. In the face of reductionism and genetic control, what does it mean to be human?

TESTING FOR GENETIC DISEASES

We already confront the challenge of genetic information in the tests that diagnose genetic diseases. In chapter 5 we looked at what this can mean for embryos and fetuses. In the Netherlands, where seriously ill adults and teens can be killed if they request euthanasia, the law is now being extended to babies. According to Tara Schupner, writing on Kansan.com, one Dutch physician, Dr. M. Rietdijk, was quoted as stating that "a baby should be killed whenever some physical or mental defect is discovered before or after birth."

While no one has yet suggested that newborns with genetic diseases should be killed here in the US, in New York State, for example, it is compulsory to test newborns for genetic diseases. There has been recent debate about extending the number of tests from eleven to four times that number. While these tests may have therapeutic benefits (treatments are available for some genetic diseases), every test means information goes into someone's medical record and can be pulled out later for some other purpose. One of the biggest questions we face is how to keep that information private, and who should have access to it.

Pressure to test later in life may be increasing, either from family members or, perhaps, from insurance companies. In one recent study in Australia, financial pressures were cited. If a family has a history of some disease, insurance companies can "load" premiums and make life or medical insurance much more expensive for those known to be at a higher risk of the disease. Someone may decide to be tested to see if they can avoid paying the higher premium. In many countries it is illegal for insurance companies to require such tests, although people may be required to tell insurers if they have had them. The UK, for example, bans the use of such tests by insurance companies.

But it is a complicated issue. If you discover that you have a fatal genetic condition and are likely to die young, you could pick up the

Clinton on Genetic Discrimination

We must not allow advances in genetics to become the basis of discrimination against any individual or group. We must never allow these discoveries to change the basic belief upon which our government, our society, and our system of ethics is founded — that all of us are created equal, entitled to equal treatment under the law.

PRESIDENT BILL CLINTON

phone and immediately insure your life for $10 million. If the insurance company must give you the same premium rates as everyone else, the system will slowly collapse as people will take advantage of it, forcing everyone else to pay (and many of the "healthy" will just stop paying). This example shows how misusing genetic information presents a problem on both sides – the new knowledge can be misused by everybody involved, including the patient. So setting fair public policy as tests become widely available will be complicated, especially in the US, which depends more on private insurance than many other countries.

GENES AND JOBS

What about employment? In *Gattaca*, employment discrimination runs rampant. Though genetic discrimination is technically illegal in the *Gattaca* world, the law is routinely flouted. The DNA from the envelope in which the application is submitted, or the cup of coffee drunk at an interview, can be analyzed and will reveal the candidate's genetic secrets as surely as a blood sample.

When Vincent goes to the Gattaca space center for his job interview, he is sent for a urine test. The physician completes the test and congratulates him. "But what about the interview?" he asks. "That was the interview," the physician dryly responds.

More than one thousand genetic tests are now available. In a recent study, 92 percent of those polled did not believe their employers should have access to the results of genetic tests, and the evidence indicates

Bush on Genetic Discrimination

Genetic discrimination is unfair to workers and their families. It is unjustified.... To deny employment or insurance to a healthy person only on a predisposition violates our country's belief in equal treatment and individual merit.

PRESIDENT GEORGE W. BUSH

these concerns are rising. People do not feel confident that such tests will not be used against them by insurers and employers.

Jane Massey Licata, a law professor from Rutgers, recently testified before a House of Representatives committee that patients worried they would lose their health insurance. A representative of the US Chamber of Commerce dismissed her concerns: "Employer collection and misuse of genetic information remains largely confined to the pages of science fiction," he said. Yet Senator Judd Gregg, usually seen as very pro-business, remained unconvinced. He steered a genetic discrimination bill through the Senate (it passed 95–0) and commented to the House committee that he had "heard from a broad range of civil rights, employment, and insurance experts, the overwhelming majority of whom agree that there are gaps in current law with respect to genetic information."

California's health insurance protections are stronger than those of many states, and "were enacted during the past 10 years after some patients hit ugly insurance snags," according to a recent report in the San Jose *Mercury News*, which tells a cautionary tale: "In 1994 Doris Goldman's family was one of the first tested for inherited Long QT Syndrome, a dangerous irregular heart rhythm. Her two adult children, Jack and Sharon, had recently died of sudden cardiac arrest. Doctors decided to test Goldman's relatives, including her grandson Jacob, born five months before her daughter's death in 1991. The tests revealed that 37 members of Goldman's family, including Jacob, carried the Long QT gene. When Jacob's father decided to start his own

The Start of a Scandal

The first documented cases in health insurance genetic discrimination date back to the 1970s when insurance companies charged African Americans carrying the gene for sickle-cell anemia a higher rate or even refused to provide coverage. Employers then used the information to deny employment, even if the carriers were perfectly healthy at the time and there was no proof that they would in fact develop the disease.

HILLARY AUGUST

business, the little boy was denied individual coverage.... State law-makers came to her aid. Jacob's full insurance was restored in 1996."

A "GENOIST" FUTURE?

Christians need not applaud all the changes of the past half century, but our society has made great strides in tackling some of the evils of discrimination. The civil rights movement offered a vigorous reasser-tion of the equal dignity of people of all races. Much of what is called feminism has been nothing more than a reminder that women, as well as men, are made in the image of God – a reminder that our culture has needed to hear. The Americans with Disabilities Act marked an enormous milestone on the road to a recognition that the strongest and the weakest are alike persons, and that we should make great efforts to enable those with disabilities to play as full a part in the human com-munity as their gifts and skills let them.

So it's a sobering thought that as we enter the "biotech century," a new and especially ugly kind of discrimination is rearing its head, a new "ism" to add to "racism." In *Gattaca* it is called "genoism," and it dehumanizes those with "strong genes" by expecting too much of them, and those with "weak genes" by expecting too little. Alongside the abortion of the handicapped, the prospect of designer babies, the patenting of genes, and (if the biotech industry gets its way) embryos, it is set to take us further down the path to a new eugenics, in which people are treated like things.

It all boils down to the person.

Personhood begins at conception. Many in the stem cell debate argue that an embryo is not a human person until it is "out of the uterus," while others argue that it is not a human person until it is "in the uterus." My friend, Christopher Hook of the Mayo Clinic, states, "These arguments based on an individual's *location* are feeble attempts to deny what has been accepted by scientists for many generations: human-hood begins with the union of twenty-three chromosomes from the ovum and twenty-three chromosomes from the sperm."

If people walking around can be discriminated against, then believe me, people like me in wheelchairs can be also. And if people with disabilities suffer from discrimination, then Lord help the tiny person in a woman's womb! But our society doesn't ascribe an embryo with the mantle of personhood.

Professor Allen Verhey of Hope College in Holland, Michigan, sees a parallel between the parable of the Good Samaritan and the debate over personhood. "The questions 'Who is a person?' and 'Who is a neighbor?' both have the same goal — to find out where our moral duties and responsibilities end. Jesus doesn't give a set of criteria to define who is a neighbor — in the same way, we can't 'invent' a set of criteria to define who is a person."

Whether you believe the soul inhabits a tiny human embryo — which I'm convinced it does — is almost beside the point. The fact is, it's *human*. It's not a goat or a rat or a chicken embryo. It is human, and each of us began our journey on this planet as one of those embryos. Life, even that small, is owed all the legal and moral protection that any human life enjoys. Life for a person that tiny — *especially* that tiny — must be protected against discrimination.

JONI

CHAPTER 10

A NEW SLAVERY

I will never forget the first day of my honeymoon as Ken and I headed to Hawaii. When he carried me across the threshold of the airplane, the flight attendant directed us to the first row of seats, away from the view of the few other passengers in first class. We got lots of special treatment: a surprise cake, Hawaiian leis, and orange juice served in crystal glasses on a silver tray. Everyone on board must have known that it was our first full day as a married couple. We snuggled down into the high backs of our comfortable seats for the long flight to the islands.

After about an hour in the air, a flight attendant reached for our window shade and said, "We're about ready to begin the movie." Ken pushed our seats back, put the earphones on me, stuffed a pillow between us, and we got ready for the film. The cabin became dark and the credits began to roll. Not but a few feet in front of my face appeared the large letters of the movie title: *Whose Life Is It Anyway?* Immediately, I recognized it as the film about a despondent quadriplegic who hates his life in a wheelchair.

The dialogue details his argument with his family and doctor to let him die. He argues that he has the right to do with his body as he wishes, even if it means insisting that three grams of phenobarbital be injected into his veins. *What a depressing film! And what an awful thing to be hit with on the first day of our marriage.* One of the flight attendants returned to apologize with a sympathetic, "And here it is your honeymoon!"

I really wasn't bothered by the incident. I know to whom my life belongs. *Whose Life Is It Anyway?* came to mind, however, when I pondered the topic of this chapter. The biotech industry wants to be able to own human beings. They have already patented genes; now they want to be able to patent human embryos and fetuses on which they have experimented. It begs the question: Whose life *is* it anyway?

When biotech enthusiasts and overzealous researchers sniff progress, watch out! Back in the sixties when I first became paralyzed, I languished in the hospital for months with nowhere to go — a bed in the local state institution had not yet become available (there were no rehab units in Maryland back then and doctors saw no hope for me). During that time, a pulmonary research specialist wanted to perform several tests on me. The gains for research seemed laudable, but when my parents learned it would involve certain drugs, they said no. We shook our heads, wondering what other patients did with no families or advocates to speak for them.

Biotech experts tend to encroach when life appears vulnerable, weak, or of little value. Perhaps it's an elitist mentality. Perhaps it's the rare air of cutting-edge research that makes them giddy, makes them feel absolved from wrongdoing, or convinces them their actions are beyond scrutiny.

My brush with research occurred back in the sixties. Today, it's a different story. A more dangerous story — if research cannot be performed on hapless quadriplegics, then let it be performed on human embryonic, fetal, or newborn life. When it comes to owning human flesh, fools rush in where angels fear to tread.

Second Corinthians 5:15 – 16 states, "And he died for all, that those who live should no longer live for themselves but for him who died for them and was raised again. So from now on *we regard no one from a worldly point of view*" (emphasis added).

We know whose life it is, anyway.

We are God's.

JONI

As the world celebrated Jonas Salk's invention of a vaccine for the terrible scourge of polio back in 1955, legendary American journalist Edmund R. Murrow asked the Nobel laureate, "Who has the patent on this vaccine?" Salk's reply is almost as famous as his vaccine. "Well, the people, I would say. There is no patent. Can you patent the sun?"

Things have changed, and are changing fast. As law professor Lori B. Andrews has shown in her book *Future Perfect*, it was during the

1980s that the life sciences, and genetics in particular, shifted from "a public interest activity to a commercial one." This represented a huge change. Governments and universities have traditionally funded science, and scientists have felt eager to publish their results—not least, as a way to build their reputations and advance their scientific careers. This has radically changed, with a shift into the private sector of growing areas of research and development, especially in the life sciences.

Some biology professors have become multimillionaires, and many others entertain hopes that they will soon be able to join them. They sit on the boards of biotech companies, and thanks to the so-called "technology transfer" laws, their universities are now strongly motivated to develop their inventions commercially and then give professors a cut of the profits (typically 30 percent). In this way, universities pull in well over one billion dollars each year.

This may or may not be bad, but it *is* new and *is* reshaping the way in which both science and business are being done, as well as giving scientists themselves big motivation and equivalent resources to try and shape science policy. Meanwhile, key changes in the way in which the patent law operates have begun to cast a long shadow over the ethics of this new situation, especially in relation to what can now be "owned" by companies and individuals.

Lawyers refer to this as "intellectual property." Just as you can own a house, you can own a trademark, or an invention (called a patent), or a song (called a copyright). If they belong to you, within limits you can do what you like with them. You can sell them; you can prevent others from using them; or you can require people to pay you whatever you can get for the privilege.

In principle this is a very good idea, and it goes all the way back to the US Constitution and before. It means that people receive encouragement to come up with new ideas, and once others get to hear about them, they can't simply help themselves. When people come up with really good ideas that everyone wants or needs (like Microsoft's software, or songs by the Beatles), huge amounts of money can change hands, and those who own the rights can become extraordinarily wealthy as people need to pay them for the privilege—often very small sums, but in very large numbers.

Patenting the Sun?

Why does this matter? Because, starting with a decision of the US Supreme Court in 1980, the trend has been to grant "intellectual property" rights to scientists and businesses over slices of the natural world. In a landmark case in 1980, the Supreme Court granted a patent on a lowly form of life – a bacterium. This surprised many people, since it had been widely assumed that because patents are issued only on "inventions," and exclude "products of nature," the life of natural organisms would remain beyond the reach of such claims.

It did not stop there: the 1980 decision led directly to the patenting of human genes, which enabled those who had identified the gene to claim it as their own – and require royalties, for example, on tests and treatments that used the gene.

While this may seem bizarre to the outsider, it has become standard practice. Some genes in your body and mine "belong" to someone else, as you will find out if you ever want to test them.

Consider a few examples of the way things are moving.

The University of Texas's famous M. D. Anderson cancer center has patented dogs – sick beagles, made sick for experimental purposes with radiation. After a public challenge by an animal welfare organization, the embarrassed university decided to abandon the patent.

In October 2000, the *Washington Post* reported: "An inventor can talk about building a better mousetrap. But, five years ago, scientists announced that they had built a better mouse – and had patented it. The new breed, dubbed PDAPP, was genetically engineered to develop signs of Alzheimer's disease, giving scientists a valuable tool for understanding the disease and testing new ideas for treatments." But soon the company was taken over by another that did not let anyone use their mice. When a researcher developed a similar mouse of his own, he could not use it to test drugs or find treatments, as it would infringe the patent and therefore be illegal. And the threat of lawsuits is real: in 1999 Elan Pharmaceuticals, who held the patent on the original mouse, sued the Mayo Foundation when it developed mice it considered similar.

Two years later, an advocacy group uncovered a patent held by the University of Missouri that describes a method of making cloned animals; it also lays claim to "the cloned products produced by these methods." This particular patent does not use language that makes clear it is not applied to humans. The *Post* comments that, "There is no specific law that excludes clones or other genetically modified human beings from being covered by patents. Some legal experts feel that constitutional law, particularly the 13th Amendment's prohibition of slavery, would rule out human patents. But others are doubtful."

Meanwhile, the *New York Times* reported on what it described as a case of "*Brave New World* meets the Marx Brothers." The European Patent Office in Munich had, by accident, it seems, slipped through a patent on the cloning of a human being that "may have granted scientists the right to change the genetic makeup of the entire human species." The *Times* comments:

> Patents have long been issued by governments, granting the exclusive right to profit from commercially applicable inventions. Biopatents, however, are recent and are largely based on one laboratory mouse. In 1988, Harvard University patented the first "transgenic" animal, a genetically altered mouse predisposed to getting cancer. After a patent moratorium in the United States ended in 1993, biotech investors turned bullish on brave new mice (and cows, pigs, and, most famously, Dolly, the cloned sheep) because of biopatents.

So human genes already have been patented and human clones may have been patented by accident. Laws intended to encourage invention have been used to make private claims on parts of our bodies (and many other creatures). The dividing line between people and property is getting blurred, and as the financial rewards from these technologies grow, the pressure is on to defend human life from being turned into a commodity.

Patents have already been issued by accident on human beings, both in the US and in Europe. And no US law prevents their being issued deliberately. In fact, after the 1980 Supreme Court case that allowed the patenting of a bacterium, despite the policy of the Patent and Trademark Office (which opposed issuing the patent), there has been growing concern that the courts could overturn another internal PTO policy—against patenting human beings.

THE WELDON AMENDMENT

In response, Dr. Dave Weldon, the congressman who has taken a lead in the House of Representatives in seeking a ban on all human cloning, introduced a modest amendment into the appropriations process that provides funding for the federal government. Using a technique that uses control of the purse strings to affect how money gets spent, Dr. Weldon proposed an amendment to the bill that funded the Patent and Trademark Office that would make it illegal to use federal dollars to issue patents on human organisms. On the floor of the House, Dr. Weldon argued that, "Technology can be used to undermine what is meant to be human."

So in an attempt to limit the distortion of human dignity for profit, through the patent system, his amendment stated, "None of the funds appropriated or otherwise made available under the act may be used to issue patents on claims directed to or encompassing a human organism." As the Patent and Trademark Office cannot issue patents apart from funds allotted during the appropriations process, the amendment essentially functioned as a ban on the patenting of human organisms as products of cloning or any other biotech process.

While hailing the great benefits in health and knowledge that accrue to society through biotechnological advances, Weldon cautioned that the pace of developments, coupled with the dynamite of "rogue scientists" who refuse to place ethical restraints upon their research, demands a collective response. Noting that the monopoly of patent protection, once granted, lasts for twenty years, Weldon asserted that Congress should take immediate action to ensure that our nation would not bestow upon researchers an opportunity to gain financially by an "exclusive right to practice such ghoulish research." Weldon called upon Congress to affirm the existing (bipartisan) policy of the PTO against granting patents on human beings at any stage of development. Weldon reassured his colleagues that the amendment would not bear upon stem cell research or gene patenting, but only on "human organisms, human embryos, human fetuses, or human beings."

The Bush administration gave its support to the Weldon amendment in the form of a letter from the director of the PTO, which stated it would welcome the support of law for its policy of refusing patents on embryos. But when the bill got to the Senate, it ran into sustained lobbying by the Biotechnology Industry Organization (BIO), the trade group of biotech companies (which also has lobbied hard against a comprehensive cloning ban). BIO and its various affiliates called on citizens and researchers to lobby their senator and stop the amendment from going through, and senators received a barrage of emails and calls from people who had been told that the Weldon Amendment would "prevent cures" for diseases. Meanwhile, BIO claimed the right to patent embryos that had been created through "human intervention," specifically including a "genetically modified embryo."

BIO's lawyers and lobbyists pressed hard through their allies in the Senate to have the amendment removed from the bill, but it had the support of the Republican leadership in House and Senate, and gained approval in the conference committee where House and Senate members come together.

As Richard Doerflinger, biotech expert at the US Conference of Catholic Bishops, said: "Unethical researchers and biotechnology companies are willing not only to create and destroy embryonic human beings for research purposes, but even to patent these fellow humans

Scientists or Businessmen?

One prominent journalist has criticized the media for the way in which they still quote "scientists" as if they were independent commentators rather than, in many cases, corporate executives who happen to be biologists too. Writing in *Washington Monthly* magazine, Neil Munro suggests that, "By keeping one foot in business and one in the university, these scientist-businessmen get the best from both worlds. As academics, they get plaudits from their peers … not to mention federally subsidized laboratory space and an endless supply of underpaid graduate students eager to help develop the next cutting-edge idea. As entrepreneurs, they get access to wealth and the investment capital needed to launch a first, second, or third company."

Munro gives as an example Irving Weissman, the Stanford professor who has played a huge role in advocating "therapeutic cloning" embryo stem cell research. "Weissman has already made millions of dollars through three companies he's founded – Systemix Inc., Celltrans Inc., and StemCells Inc., the last two of which he still helps manage – which use the stem cell technology. When President Bush announced last August that he would give narrow support to such technology, the market value of StemCells Inc. briefly shot up by 45 percent."

so they can license, market, buy, and sell them as mere commodities." He added: "By prohibiting patents on human organisms, Congress has helped prevent such gross abuses and has taken some of the profit motive out of the drive for human cloning."

Its importance is underlined by a far-sighted report in the *Wall Street Journal* back in 2001. After noting that "ethical prohibitions embodied in patent law in the US and Europe are preventing scientists from securing patents on some pioneering biological inventions," science reporters Antonio Regalado and Meera Louis say this: "These applications are testing legal limits and setting the stage for what many expect will be an eventual legal challenge to allow patents to cover human reproductive cloning as well."

As we survey what lies ahead, we begin to see why "intellectual property" issues are so vital. Bioscience is becoming more and more part of the corporate life of the world, and profit-seeking scientists and entrepreneurs together need to be given a clear message: *human life is not a commodity.* The law already has gone much too far in allowing patents on human genes. It has, only just, been held back from issuing patents on human embryos. The question of who owns what, and what may never be owned, goes to the heart of the struggle for human dignity that will determine the course of the twenty-first century.

I'll never forget the day I visited the Nazi concentration camps of Auschwitz and Birkenau. Even though the grounds of the death camps looked tidy with wispy wildflowers around the base of their brick buildings, they were depressing places.

When I noticed a row of rosebushes planted yards away from the gas chambers, our guide quickly pointed out that where the flowers are, once there was hard, naked clay, with every blade of grass picked clean by starving prisoners. I looked around and could easily imagine the barbed wire and the guard towers, the ominous chimneys rising above ovens and the rows of barracks.

My husband Ken helped lift me in my wheelchair up the few steps to the museum. Once inside, I slowly wheeled past the displays of eyeglasses and hair. Then another display caught my eye. Behind the glass I saw piles of leg braces attached to shoes, canes, crutches, and hearing aids. Next to the piles lay stacks of yellowed, dusty record books which neatly tabulated the names and numbers of thousands of disabled people.

I shivered. Not so much from the cold as from the thought that people disabled just like me were the first to be exterminated, labeled as "useless bread gobblers." Hitler's strategy to eradicate people with disabilities progressed in stages. First it was compulsory sterilization; then a formal killing operation, known as Aktion T4, quickly followed. More than 275,000 disabled people were murdered in the T4 program, not counting those killed in institutions after the program ended and those in occupied countries. The Nazis especially targeted disabled children—untold numbers perished in institutions governed by the T4 program. Nazi

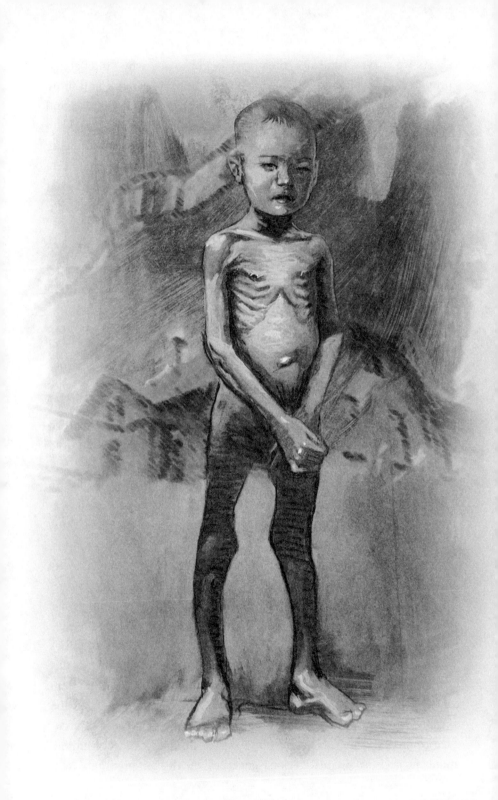

PART THREE: TREATING PEOPLE LIKE THINGS

ideology considered disability a sign of degeneracy. A sign of weakness. An open passport to abuse.

The horror took place years ago. But don't think it couldn't happen again!

In Indiana, an infant with Down syndrome was denied simple surgery and starved and dehydrated to death; two judges declined to stop the abuse. A medical team in Oklahoma used a "quality of life" formula to urge nontreatment for babies with spina bifida—a formula that meant most of the families so urged were poor and uneducated. Twenty-four babies died, most from untreated infections. No criminal charges were ever filed against the medical team. It reminds me of Proverbs 17:15, "Acquitting the guilty and condemning the innocent—the LORD detests them both."

Our age invites us to embrace policies that devalue human life. I see a direct connection between removing a brain-injured woman from her feeding tube, to the use of human embryos in stem cell research, to the patenting of people's genes.

The moral vacuum of the Nazi death camps held the seeds of our twenty-first century utilitarian medicine. Look at what Willard Gaylin, M.D., a doctor and renowned bioethicist, stated in *Harpers Magazine*: "Preventive medicine drives up the ultimate cost of healthcare to society by enlarging the population of the elderly and infirm. The child who would have died from polio will grow up to be a very expensive old man or woman.... Good medicine keeps sick people alive, thereby increasing the number of sick people in the population." Note how money influences medical policy. It's 1 Timothy 6:10, "For the love of money is a root of all kinds of evil."

Earlier generations would never have sanctioned the patenting of people's genes—indeed, patenting people. Harvesting organs from unborn humans, designing babies, and using computers to enhance people's physical and mental abilities *does not* enjoy universal support or agreement, even in many secular societies. That alone should cause us to pause. It alone should cause any thinking person to rise up!

This is not a battle between "progressives" and "religious conserva-tives." More than twenty-five national disability advocacy groups are campaigning vigorously against the further devaluing of human life; they realize their own lives are in jeopardy.

God has a heart for the weak and vulnerable. He has a heart for the unborn. He tells us in Psalm 82:3 to "Defend the cause of the weak and fatherless; maintain the rights of the poor and oppressed. Rescue the weak and needy; deliver them from the hand of the wicked." Look at those verbs: *defend, maintain, rescue,* and *deliver.* They are clarion calls for action.

The media and the medical community, the biotech industry and the "progressives" try to disguise their policies with rosebush arguments and wildflower words. But they can't cover up the hard, naked fact. "There is a way that seems right to a man, but in the end it leads to death" (Proverbs 14:12).

And not just the death of those people who are patented! It'll be the death of humanity.

JONI

CHAPTER 11

FAKING LIFE

This chapter reminds me of an old Sunday school lesson.

It was back in the fifties, but I can still smell the lemon oil on the wooden desks and see the glow of morning sun on the stained-glass windows. I can hear the wooden floors creak and the strains of the choir singing in the next room. A picture of Jesus hangs on the wall, one with lambs and children. Crayon-colored Josephs and King Davids adorn the corkboard. It was St. Paul's United Methodist Church in the rural village of Sykesville ... a scene from a bygone era.

Our Sunday school lesson sounded like something from a bygone era too. It highlighted an obscure passage in Genesis 6:4 – 5: "The Nephilim were on the earth in those days — and also afterward — when the sons of God went to the daughters of men and had children by them. They were the heroes of old, men of renown. The LORD saw how great man's wickedness on the earth had become, and that every inclination of the thoughts of his heart was only evil all the time."

Our Sunday school teacher explained that when the daughters of men married the "sons of God" — the Nephilim — they produced offspring who were inhuman. Different. Strange. Offspring not of the human race. My teacher further explained that this may have been one of the main reasons God wiped humans off the face of the earth with the Great Flood; it was the only way to ensure that this strange, aberrant race of quasi-humans would be eradicated. It seemed logical to me, for Genesis 6:6 – 7 went on to say, "The LORD was grieved that he had made man on the earth, and his heart was filled with pain. So the LORD said, 'I will wipe mankind, whom I have created, from the face of the earth.'"

God didn't destroy everyone, however. "The LORD then said to Noah, 'Come into the ark, you and your whole family, because I have found you righteous in this generation.... Seven days from now I will send rain on the earth forty days and forty nights, and I will wipe from the face of the earth every living creature I have made'" (Genesis 7:1, 4). God rescued that which he created, animals and humans. *Real* humans.

I completely forgot about that Sunday school lesson until a year ago when I traveled to a Midwest college campus to attend a conference called "What Does It Mean to Be Human?" The lecturers presented shocking material. Each presenter showed graphs, photos, and quotes underscoring that researchers are now manipulating atoms in a whole new area of science called nanotechnology. Soon, these designer atoms will seamlessly weave their way into the brains and muscles of a select group of people. They will be a breed apart from most humans, advanced in intellect and excelling in health, strength, and longevity. In the not-too-distant future we will live alongside what the lecturers called *transhumans*.

Or perhaps ... Nephilim.

JONI

"If a monkey is hungry but has his arms pinned, there's not much he can do about it. Unless that monkey can control a nearby robotic arm with his brain. And that's exactly what the monkey in Andrew Schwartz's neurology lab at the University of Pittsburgh can do, feeding himself using a prosthetic arm controlled solely by his thoughts." So David Cohn in *Wired* magazine reports on the latest developments in connecting the brain and machines powered by brainwaves.

But connections between brains and machines have not been confined to monkeys. Kevin Warwick, author of *I, Cyborg*, claims to be the world's first "cybernetic organism" and has been busy experimenting on himself—and on his wife. According to a recent report in the *New Zealand Herald*, "When Kevin Warwick lifted his finger, his wife Irena felt as if a bolt of lighting ran down her palm and into her own finger. In what they billed as the first direct link between nervous systems, the couple had electrodes surgically implanted in their arms and linked by radio signals to a computer."

We began by noting that the biggest issue confronting the human race in this new century is the need to treat people like people, and things like things. God made us in his image to rule over other creatures, and we must do so responsibly as his stewards. Others made

in his image, whatever their age, however healthy or diseased they may be, whether religious or not, of all nations and tribes – everyone is made with dignity given by God, and that is how we must treat them.

The final stage in our tour of the threats to human dignity comes from a different source. So far, we have been talking about biology, and especially about the dangers of turning the body, or parts of it, into "commodities." We have focused on how close we are to designing our babies, and using genetic engineering to change human nature itself by adding "enhancements" and in the process turning ourselves into things we have made. We laid out the threefold challenge of bioethics, starting with the taking of life (abortion, euthanasia) and the making of life (genetics, cloning). Now we come to the third: the faking of life, in which machines are used to "enhance" our human nature and change it into something else.

We've all seen the movies. How can we forget Robin Williams's charm in *Bicentennial Man*, as the robot who asks to be accepted as a human being, and finally chooses to die since it is the human thing to do? Or Spielberg's *AI*, in which "orga" and "mecha" – the organic and the mechanical – come together as a robot sibling seeks his "mother's" love, only to be despised by the real son?

This is not completely new. The blurring of human and machine is an old story; Frankenstein was a manmade monster. What *is* new is a combination of new technology (some of these options could soon work), and the charm offensive. Can anyone be less like *Frankenstein* than Robin Williams? (How would *Bicentennial Man* have scored at the box office had Williams's part been played by old-time horror actor Vincent Price?) Or to shift gears, has there been a children's toy less threatening than a Tamagochi – the feed-me, hold-me, computer pets of the nineties?

Yet all is not sweetness and light. Science fiction is fast becoming science fact. Is that also true here? And if so, how should we view it?

BILL JOY'S CHALLENGE

Bill Joy, cofounder and chief technologist for Sun Microsystems, has said that our computing power may increase by a factor of one million in the next thirty years. If that proves true, or even only partly true (what would a merely thousand times more powerful PC be able to do?), it means we must begin to think ahead very seriously. Because "artificial intelligence" ("AI" as it is known) is on the march, and no one suggests that computers will get *less* powerful.

Experts already are seriously debating whether AI will ever rival human intelligence. Some say yes and welcome it, others answer yes and fear it, and still others say no. Whichever group is right, every year brings us machines more capable of approximating human responses. Voice-recognition programs already give us voice dialing on our cell phones and in the telephone answering systems of credit card companies and airlines. Things are moving fast.

Selmer Bringsjord is a leading thinker on artificial intelligence and a strong proponent of the view that AI will never be able to take the place of human intelligence. "I'll happily wager the value of my retirement savings in, say, 2030, that what I will be able to accomplish then on an average workday will be utterly beyond the smartest computing machine available that year.... To sit down with a pen before a blank piece of paper and produce a play like *Hamlet* involves doing something that no computer, however fast, can pull off."

Bill Joy's warning appeared in a famous article published in *Wired*, the techie magazine. It is one of the most strident statements yet made about the threats to human nature posed by technology. And while statements of that kind have been made many times by environmentalists and other activists, to have their concerns echoed by one of the gurus of the technological age was remarkable.

Bill Joy's article had the arresting title "Why the Future Doesn't Need Us." He began by listing three great threats to human existence in the twentieth century: chemical, biological, and nuclear warfare. By contrast, he argued, in the twenty-first century, the threats will become far more sophisticated: genetics, artificial intelligence, and nanotechnology. These technologies will likely have one of two outcomes, says Joy. Either through some terrible mistake they will destroy humankind. Or, alternatively, they will "destroy" us in another way, by blending human and machine and ultimately superseding human nature with a machine nature that uses some combination of these technologies. So through a disaster or a series of bad choices, we will end up saying goodbye to human nature.

Side by side with the question of AI machines is that of the development of connections between AI machines and human beings. The word *cyborg* describes the result: a *cyb*ernetic *org*anism, or cyb-org. In many ways, this is more troubling. The idea that the human brain could be connected with machine implants that would alter its functioning is very disturbing. And lest we think such a scenario remains far off, we must realize that experiments aiming at this very thing are going on right now.

Robots and Us

This chapter cannot give more than a summary of some of the issues that we shall soon have to face. For, alongside genetics, the "cyborg" future of artificial intelligence and nanotechnology will put the unique dignity of a human being under growing pressure.

It ought to disturb us that some key thinkers in this field very candidly declare their goals: to eradicate the distinction between the human and the mechanical—the "mecha" and "orga" of Spielberg's film *AI: Artificial Intelligence*—and develop what they have called the "singularity," in which organic and mechanical become one. We need to grasp what is happening, and then begin to reflect deeply on a Christian response.

They Say We Are "Human-Racists"

What's our goal? The bioLuddites and human-racists are already in place. They control the bully pulpit of the President's Council on Bioethics, and they have their mediagenic talking heads, their think tanks, foundation grants, journals, and lobbyists. They are organizing conferences for devout Christians, radical Greens, and suburban soccer moms. They have filled the media with alarmist rhetoric.

James Hughes, *Transhumanist*

Let's look at the big picture. We know that much of what we do can be done equally well or better by machines. In fact, the whole idea of technology, from primitive tools onward, is the story of our making things that enable us to do more than we could without them. So it's no great surprise that clever machines have been devised that copy what we do and even do it better.

Those of us old enough to have used both typewriters and computers have discovered that word processing is much more like longhand writing than typing is. Typing places words into instant, permanent form. (Some of us remember the agonies of erasing type, especially when we had five carbon copies in the typewriter.) Writing by hand on paper, you can scribble and scratch and constantly make small and large changes—just like we can on a computer. Technology really can develop intuitive applications, some of which made this book much easier to write.

The idea of the "robot" is just the same: making a machine that aids us in doing what we do anyway, doing it quicker or more accurately or cheaper. We've all seen pictures of robot vacuum cleaners, though they have yet to become a commercial success, because cleaning a house is rather complicated. We have seen the industrial robots used to put cars and other complex machines together. None of this worries us, even though at every point these machines are copying and often perfecting what we normally do ourselves.

The advent of the computer has raised the stakes in the debate about humans and technology. Now we have attached a "brain" to the mechanical devices that, though complicated, essentially have been spades and hammers and paintbrushes on poles. What are the implications for human dignity if these "machines" prove able to do *everything* that we do?

This raises three sets of issues.

First, the technology debate: what *can* be done, and what do the experts think will soon be possible? Surprise! They disagree. Some believe we will be able to duplicate everything humans can do, all the way to creating works of art—and even do it better. Others think that that will never be possible, and that merely having faster computers does not mean the ability to replicate the human mind.

Can We "Improve" on Being Human?

The National Science Foundation's 2002 report on *Converging Technologies for Improving Human Performance* — concerned with nanotechnology and its "convergence" with biotechnology, information technology, and cognitive science — flirts with the transhumanist agenda.

They offer examples of research goals and anticipated results: "enhancing individual sensory and cognitive capacities ... improving both individual and group creativity ... communication techniques including brain-to-brain interaction, perfecting human-machine interfaces including neuromorphic engineering" (p. ix). They ask, "How can we develop a transforming national strategy to enhance individual capacities and overall societal outcomes? What should be done to achieve the best results over the next 10 to 20 years?" And, at the end of one list of long-term implications, they designate "Human evolution, including individual and cultural evolution" (p. 4). "Technological convergence could become the framework for human convergence. The twenty-first century could end in world peace, universal prosperity, and evolution to a higher level of compassion and accomplishment" (p. 6). "[I]t may be that humanity would become like a single, distributed and interconnected 'brain' based in new core pathways of society" (p. 6).

Second, what are some people *trying* to accomplish? What are the goals of those either working with these clever machines, or cheering them on and discussing what they are doing? We've already mentioned words like *transhumanist*. These people believe that these technologies will enable us to add to human powers and, eventually, replace human nature itself with something better. We start with memory chips for our brains, and end up in the famous sci-fi scenario in which our conscious essence gets "uploaded" into computers and we continue life without the disadvantages inherent in a biological species. This, at the moment, is a fringe movement, comprised mainly of philosophers who like to theorize about it. But some engineers and scientists are eager to "improve" on human nature, piece by piece.

Third, we have the question: what does this matter to us? Christians believe that one can't "improve" on human nature, because we bear God's image. That does not mean, of course, that we don't need medicine; and every effort at enabling sick and handicapped people to enjoy a fuller experience of being human is wonderful. But if it goes beyond that and breaks out of "being human" into some other kind of being, human technology has run far out of control.

Lines will not be easy to draw.

Someone whose brain has been damaged by a fall should, perhaps, have the benefit of a microchip that gives him or her back a normal, functioning human brain. But the same chip, implanted in someone who has not had a fall, in theory could give the person "superhuman" brain function. If you want to ace your SATs, should you be able to buy a chip that will do the trick and avoid all that revision? If you want to pass the bar exam, or qualify as a pharmacist, should you be able to buy a chip? Those options may sound shocking and subhuman, not superhuman.

IS GENE DOPING OUR FUTURE?

We may find the best illustration of this problem in doping and sports. Most people agree that doping doesn't make athletes better athletes, into supermen and superwomen. It means they cease to be athletes at all; they become subhuman. It isn't simply that sports will be over if doping can't be controlled (and if it can't, it will become a competition between teams of chemists), but human nature will be over. When you get strong muscles by popping steroids rather than working out, you have begun to trade your human dignity for the dignity of a machine.

The most worrying development, which shows how fast the technology is moving, lies in the prospect of using genetic engineering for "doping." The *Boston Globe* recently reported that a monkey researcher had accidentally discovered how to make a "supermonkey." Dr. Jim Wilson of the University of Pennsylvania inserted into monkey muscle cells a gene that boosts levels of a hormone that manufactures red blood cells. "In less than two weeks, many of Wilson's rhesus monkeys had red-cell counts greater than those of world-class runners who train at high altitude." Wilson's monkeys all died – a warning of the hazards of genetics – and it was Wilson whose experiments on humans later led to the death of eighteen-year-old Jesse Gelsinger in a clinical trial that tried a genetics cure for his liver condition.

Asking the question, "Will athletes go for the ultimate high?" Christen Brownlee in *Science News* notes that H. Lee Sweeney, a pioneering researcher on mouse muscle enhancement, has been deluged with calls. "Soon, the calls and e-mails started flowing in, first as a trickle, then as if from a fire hose.... Some people beg him to reverse their muscle degeneration caused by disease or aging. However, around half of the calls and e-mails come from healthy individuals – professional power lifters, sprinters, and weekend wannabe athletes of all stripes. They want bigger, higher-performing muscles. One caller offered him $100,000 for muscle enhancement, and a high school football coach asked Sweeney to treat his whole team."

But what if you are a pastor, and a chip comes out that would mean you had the whole of the Bible immediately available to your memory? What about when Christian publishers make their latest titles available in paper, CD, and brain chip versions? It will be hard to say no to some of these options, for the same reason that it is always hard to resist temptation! Temptation is always attractive. And the temptation to do one better than God – to become superhuman by adding computer chips and using genetic engineering to enhance the species – may be the hardest temptation we sinners ever have to face.

Sometimes in those twilight hours when I can't sleep, or occasionally in my more ethereal moments, I wonder what will happen. I wonder when the patience of God will come to an end.

I can't say. We eat, drink, marry, and raise families, all with barely a nano-thought as to how nanotechnology will affect our world. It still seems like science fiction. We have loan applications to fill out, kids to drive to karate, birthday gifts to buy, retirements to plan, and grandchildren to make scrapbooks for. But then I read verses like Matthew 24:37 – 40, "As it was in the days of Noah, so it will be at the coming of the Son of Man. For in the days before the flood, people were eating and drinking, marrying and giving in marriage, up to the day Noah entered the ark; and they knew nothing about what would happen until the flood came and took them all away. That is how it will be at the coming of the Son of Man."

Wait a minute. *How* will it be at the coming of the Son of Man? The time when we finally cross the line of God's patience? It will be as in the days of Noah. As in the days of those strange, abnormal people, the Nephilim.

It's just a wild guess and I really don't care to go down that dark, grim path. I would rather relegate the dismantling of our world to, well … a bygone era. Rather than plow ahead into the brash, bizarre world of transhumans, I would prefer to stave off the end of the age by easing back on the edge of God's patience. I want to — and I believe you want to — season our culture with the salt of truth and light. We dare not become cynical, uninvolved, or indifferent. As someone has said, "The salt of the earth does not mock rotting meat. Where it can, it saves and seasons. And where it can't, it weeps. And the light of the world does not withdraw, saying 'Good riddance' to godless darkness. It labors to illuminate."

It'll make us extremely unpopular if we follow that advice. Then again, Jesus warned us in Matthew 10:22, "All men will hate you because of me, but he who stands firm to the end will be saved." Dr. John Piper has observed, "Being Christian exiles [in a technological culture] does not end our influence, it takes the swagger out of it. We don't get cranky that our country has been taken away. We don't whine about the triumphs of evil. We are not hardened with anger. We understand. This is not new. This was the way it was in the beginning — Antioch, Corinth, Athens, Rome … It never occurred to those early exiles that they should rant about the ubiquity of secular humanism. They simply saw it as a time for influence, not with huffing and puffing, but with tears and persuasion and perseverance."

We must not allow ourselves to be intimidated by an intellectual elite who insists on "progress" at the expense of the human race. To be a Christian in this brave new world, we have to shine light, shake salt, serve with longsuffering mercy, tell the truth, and keep pointing people to Jesus Christ.

After all, he is the One who is *fully* human.

Shaping the Future:
Christians Lead the *Technosapiens* Discussion

At the end of 2004, a group of approximately eighty men and women met in Washington, DC, to discuss questions that will dominate the twenty-first century. The press was not much interested, and plenty of people chose to do something else. But the audience contained a smattering of people from the federal government and various think tanks, as well as academics and lobbyists. I was privileged to chair the meeting. Our discussions proved illuminating, and their subject matter will be the theme of our children's and grandchildren's generation.

The topic was not simply the future of the human race, as we generally understand that phrase; but whether the human race *has* a future. Because the technologies that have given rise to discoveries in genetics, the cloning of animals, and the development of tiny particles and machines (nanotechnology) may soon be in a position to transform human nature itself.

The conference was called *Technosapiens?* The main sponsor of the *Technosapiens* process was the Center for Bioethics and Culture (thecbc.org), which brought together leading lights from science, policy, and philosophy. Some were Christians, some secularists. Some were conservatives, some progressives. Some—such as Nick Bostrom, founder of the World Transhumanist Association—argued that it was wonderful that these new technologies could remake human nature. Others—such as Leon Kass, chairman of the President's Council on Bioethics—took the opposite view. And, in a manner that is becoming normal, we found feminists and environmentalists side by side with conservative Christians, making the case for the integrity of human nature.

The word *Technosapiens* has been made up to underline the challenge that technology poses to human nature—*Homo sapiens*, "wise humankind"—since the logic of the latest technology is to seek to "enhance" human nature in a manner that ultimately, if it works and is not stopped, will efface the distinction between human nature and the machines humans can make.

Not many Christians are alert to these issues. Yet many of us believe that they will dominate the twenty-first century, and how we decide them will determine the kind of beings we become. Of course, only the extremists will say out loud, "We want to remake human nature." Most of those who favor unrestricted development of technology simply say it is inevitable, or it will produce cures for diseases, or it will give us incremental improvements that we can use to help others. There are dozens of "good" arguments: we have seen some of them deployed, disingenuously but effectively, in the debates about embryo stem cell research and cloning. The problem is that nowhere has the saying been truer that the road to hell is paved with good intentions (or, at least, arguments that sound well intended).

So what do we do? We need to note two key principles. First, let's understand the issues. Use the resources that some of us have produced so you can get up to speed, in your homes and schools and churches. We must be the best-informed people around.

Second, we need to get into debate. We will find strange bedfellows, and let's welcome their help. We will find ourselves opposing articulate exponents of the idea that we can remake human nature. The *Technosapiens* conferences have opened up the biggest questions of the century, in ways that are informed and gracious. How this debate concludes – what will happen to *Homo sapiens* in the years ahead – is in God's hands . . . and in those of his servants.

Nigel Cameron

JONI

PART FOUR

So What Can We Do?

Whether we are patients, politicians, or pastors, God calls us to be brave in the brave new world. There is something for each of us to do, and it starts here.

The biotech agenda of the brave new world involves three successive assaults on the sanctity of life that God made in his image: *taking*, *making*, and *faking*. Abortion and embryo research have so far focused on the *taking* of human life. Yet as biotech unfolds its new powers, the emphasis will move from taking life to *making* life — designing babies to order, reshaping human nature. And beyond biology, developments in fields like robotics threaten a third wave: the *faking* of life, as machines are used to enhance and change human nature itself.

This is just the beginning of the "biotech century," and God has given us a unique opportunity to shape how things unfold in the years to come. He has placed us as believers in the twenty-first century, and we need to prepare ourselves to make a difference.

Now we turn to the challenges of what lies ahead, and what to do about it with God.

"Defend the cause of the weak and fatherless; maintain the rights of the poor and oppressed. Rescue the weak and needy; deliver them from the hand of the wicked" (Psalm 82:3 – 4).

CHAPTER 12

WHAT DO WE DO NOW?

We are standing at a unique point in history. All the advances in technology that have enabled humankind to move from primitive tribal cultures to complex societies have only begun to prepare us for what comes next.

We have now begun to use technology on ourselves, to reshape ourselves, to determine what we shall be – a watershed in the history of the human race. Until now our human nature has been "given," something we inherit and take for granted. We can keep fit, eat well, use surgery and medications to address accidents and ailments. We are who we are, and who God has made us.

On the Threshold

Today we stand on the threshold of a brave new world in which it will increasingly be up to us to decide who we shall be. In small and significant ways, it already is.

Using in vitro technology with "pre-implantation genetic diagnosis" enables us to weed out genetically sick embryos and perform very early abortions. But it also enables us to choose babies whose tissue and organs we may want to use later, for others.

The cloning debate shows how things will develop. Look at this pattern: First will come some new discovery, a new technique, an amazing and disturbing achievement. It will dominate the news magazines, and in common with many others, we will worry about what it may mean. The biotech industry and its allies in the medical and science communities will lobby hard for its acceptance. New scientific discoveries usually need no law to make them legal; it is the old laws that need to be revised, and that is hard. Turning outrage and alarm into public policy will prove complex and difficult.

Those who support the new technique will hold out the prospect of "cures"; disabled and sick people will get paraded in front of congressional committees and television cameras.

Meanwhile, the biotech lobbyists will play with language and use focus groups to devise the best way to market this new "product." Sometimes they will employ an outrageous technique – as in the Harry and Louise pro-cloning radio ads, when one character asks the other (talking about embryo cloning for experiments), "Isn't this cloning?" and gets the resounding answer "Noooo!" Dr. Goebels, Hitler's propaganda chief, became famous for his declaration that lies need to be big to be believable. The biotech industry's "big lie" that denies that experimental embryo cloning is cloning at all is a terrible warning of what we shall soon face. The debasing of language will make debate increasingly hard.

Meanwhile, in our first struggle for human dignity in the face of biotechnology, we have barely made a start. Many worried Christians have moved to the forefront of the campaign to ban cloning. Yet most others fail to see the importance of the issue or know much about it. Fewer still understand that this is just the tip of the biotech iceberg. An agenda awaits us that will rival and surpass the significance of abortion. The human species is in the process of redesign and reinvention; the "post-human future" awaits us.

In his famous book commending a Christian view of all of life, Francis Schaeffer asked the question, *How Should We Then Live?* How are we to live as believers in the first years of the twenty-first century? How are we to live, knowing what we know about the mix of blessings and threats that come together in the biotech revolution – and the profound threat that it could pose to humankind? Are these things inevitable? Can we resist them? What strategy should we use?

STRATEGIES FOR THE CHURCH: SALT AND LIGHT IN THE TWENTY-FIRST CENTURY

God calls us to be salt and light, and never before has that role been more important. We are light to declare the truth; we are salt to preserve what is good and deter decay. We are called to be salt and light in the face of biotech's threat to human nature and its unique dignity. So what do we do?

Four key strategies need to work together.

1. Be distinctive!

The apostle Paul tells us not to be "conformed" to the standards of the world around us. Never has that principle been more needed than as we face the brave new world. Just as Christians have learned to "just say no" to abortion, and as they may soon need to say no to euthanasia, we will be called on to navigate complex uses of technology as we retain our distinctive Christian identity.

We find little encouragement in how Christians have responded to in vitro fertilization. Pastors and teachers have ignored it, and many Christians have been through treatment cycles with little awareness of the huge ethical issues at stake. But the debate on cloning and embryo stem cell research has awakened us to the fact that abortion is not the only issue of profound moral significance. We are more alert to the emerging biotech agenda. If we can learn well from this experience, we will become prepared for the demands on our integrity that we will soon meet. Our discipleship may meet no greater challenges as we step forward into the vast temptations of the brave new world – temptations in the shadow of Babel.

2. Be informed!

The church of Jesus Christ must be by far the best-informed sector of the population in respect to these new questions and the threats they pose. That means education – and the church is well able to mount a huge educational initiative for its members. Only in this way will we become prepared to live distinctive lives, and to serve as salt and light for human dignity in our culture.

3. Mobilize!

We must mobilize. The energy and commitment that have characterized Christian response to abortion show what can be achieved.

Yet, as we know, political work on abortion has engaged only a small slice of the church. Many sympathize; few have acted.

We have vast potential in the church, with tens of millions of Christians and, side by side with the educational resources of individual congregations, we have hundreds of colleges, seminaries, and Bible schools; huge parachurch ministries; websites and magazines and conferences. As the biotech challenge emerges as the greatest opportunity for salt-and-light Christian response in this century, we have at our disposal a vast reservoir of resources.

4. Engage!

We must engage. As on so many great issues of the day, some outside the church agree with us, and we welcome their agreement and seek to work with them. Such a strategy was the cornerstone of William Wilberforce's famous efforts to end slavery. This eminent British statesman worked with anyone who would work with him to improve the conditions of the slaves, to end the slave trade, and finally to abolish slavery in the global British Empire a generation before the Civil War raged here in the US. We have worked with unbelievers on the rights of the handicapped, on pornography, human rights, the reform of prison conditions, and religious liberty. We must work with others here.

Most people agree with us that cloning is wrong. That includes many religious leaders—some mainline, liberal Christians (who, like the United Methodist Church, are often pro-choice on abortion), as well as Jewish and Islamic leaders, for example. It also includes many environmentalists and pro-choice feminists. Christians need to be ready to work with anyone who believes that human dignity is at stake in the biotech revolution and is prepared to work with us. It will bring us side by side with people who take very different views on other issues—what writer and lawyer Wesley Smith has called "strange clonefellows"!

Be distinctive. Be informed. Mobilize. Engage. Powerful ideas can have powerful consequences—but we must build strategies and follow through with them if we want our ideas to shape the culture. That is how we answer those many committed believers who ask us: "But what can I do?"

Sometimes the emphasis is on the "I" – "What can *I* do?" Every individual, each one of us, can commit to this fourfold challenge.

Sometimes the emphasis is on the "do" – "But what can I *do*?" People often ask that question as a way of shrugging their shoulders, throwing up their hands in horror, turning their backs, and walking away from a problem that seems too big to face. But the answer is always very practical. In the rest of this chapter we outline some practical steps we can all take, starting now. We believe in a great God who has given his people mighty resources for such a time as this. This battle is winnable. But – to stick with the metaphor of war – we must be prepared to fight.

Abortion and the Biotech Agenda

Key to the educational program that will awaken the church to the biotech agenda is our commitment to fight abortion. For a generation, abortion has captured the heart and imagination of Christians like nothing else. From a slow start, evangelicals have joined Catholics in an equal partnership in political as well as caring work. As a result, the pro-life movement has grown powerful in Washington, DC, and in state capitals around the nation. Through hundreds of crisis pregnancy centers, tens of thousands of devoted volunteers work to undermine the abortion culture in their communities. Abortion has proved the one issue of bioethics that has engaged the conscience of the church and commanded its action. Indeed, it has proved the one social issue that has captured the imagination of Christians on a huge scale. It gives a sharp focus to our political influence and has been the chief distinguishing mark of our agenda for cultural issues. We seek a culture of life.

Yet while abortion stands out as "the" issue for many Christians, fewer than desired have taken this issue seriously. In every church fellowship you can find a handful of activists. So much depends on the pastor or priest. It is not that most evangelical pastors and Catholic priests are pro-choice, but they have different priorities. They do not all agree that this issue is so important.

That is not a criticism (although that depends on their other priorities!). God does not call us to spend all our time and resources fighting abortion. Believers face many challenges in a culture that is slowly but surely turning its back on the Christian vision of the world. But in many churches, the "priorities" are inward-looking, institutional issues such as new buildings.

For many Christians, the great social and cultural issues of our day attract hardly any notice at all. *Most evangelical Christians do not even vote!* Many of them seem able to live in almost complete disengagement from the culture and its "salt and light" opportunities. Jesus told the parable of the Good Samaritan to illustrate how religious people can use their religion to block out love for their neighbors. All the vast religious activity of our generation, with its buildings and organizations and meetings, can offer us cover as we ignore the needs of our day and our opportunities to meet them. We conveniently forget that, for a Christian, every opportunity is also a responsibility.

Second, the pro-life movement has focused almost exclusively on abortion and shown little interest either in the emerging biotech issues or even the growing threat of euthanasia. Abortion, of course, is not a disease; it is a symptom. The move to liberal abortion is not an isolated development; it emerges from a much broader collapse in our idea of what it means to be human, and from a compliant and weak medical profession that has gone along with changing social assumptions. Euthanasia is a further symptom of the same disease.

When Francis Schaeffer and C. Everett Koop issued their wake-up call, *Whatever Happened to the Human Race?*—a book and a powerful video series that had a dramatic effect on evangelicals worldwide—they made exactly this point: that abortion and euthanasia are twin products of the same abandonment of the sanctity of life.

Third, as we cast our eyes on the unfolding biotech agenda, the pro-life movement's great strength—its strong focus on abortion—could also emerge as a weakness. For while abortion is a vivid example of the principle we have been discussing in every chapter—treating people like things, using human beings as commodities, denying the image of God – back of abortion lies a new mindset in medicine and society. We find ourselves in a much wider discussion in which medicine and technology are on trial. Euthanasia and cloning are not "other" issues; they form part of the same issue. And as we have been arguing all through this book, manufacturing and manipulating human life is evil in the same way that killing is evil. Abortion, for all its horror, is not *the* issue; it is merely the plainest example so far of the abuse of human dignity in our culture. But there are others. And they are getting worse.

So as we seek to educate the church, we need to begin with abortion, but not end there. What lies behind *taking* human life (abortion, euthanasia), *making* human life (the copying and manipulation of the new biotech – cloning, genetic engineering), and the prospect of *faking* life (artificial intelligence, nanotechnology) is really one principle: the desire for power and control over human life, our own and the lives of others. It is a desire for power and control to decide, not just issues of life and death, but what kind of life shall be lived. It's the Babel desire to declare independence from God and assert absolute control over us and our affairs. It's the sin of rebellion against God, let loose first in the Garden of Eden, sampled in Cain's murder of his brother, and finally demonstrated by the builders of the tower. Yet they were just preparing the way for us. What they built with bricks and mortar we build with eggs and sperm and genes and nanotechnology.

If we are to work to prevent, under God, what C. S. Lewis called "the abolition of man," these opening years of the twenty-first century are our strategic moment. We have in our generation the best opportunity for Christians to be salt and light. We have a cause so great that we find it hard to grasp its importance. We have a chance to shape the future for good and for God, and defeat forces intent on destroying human nature as we know it. Babel is rising again, a high-tech challenge to the glory of God and the dignity of his human creatures. Today's Babel builders are out to make a name for themselves on a far larger scale. God has called us to rule his earth for him. Jesus Christ has summoned us to be salt and light in the corruption of our own generation. *This* is our task.

We need to get on with it.

We wrestle not against the media, the biotech industry, and pharmaceutical companies. In this battle, we wrestle against spiritual powers of darkness.

Christians recognize the Devil as a real and personal being. Scripture calls him a liar, a murderer, and an accuser of the brethren (John 8:44; Revelation 12:10). He *lies* in that he pushes the premise that a tiny "clump of cells in a petri dish" isn't worthy of moral respect and legal safeguards. The Devil is a *murderer* in that he promotes the destruction of human life, whether in a research lab or by the bedside of a ventilator-dependent, brain-injured person. Finally, he is an *accuser of the brethren* in that he slanders Christians, charging us with caring more about "zygotes" than real people with heartbreaking diseases; he is constantly condemning Christians who work to safeguard life and promote human dignity.

At the Joni and Friends International Disability Center and the Christian Institute on Disability, we understand it is a moral battle, a battle that focuses on what people believe about the human embryo. We believe that all pursuit of medical advancements reflects *somebody's* morals; we don't want the media, politicians, celebrities, pharmaceutical companies, and the biotech industry setting the moral agenda. Wise leaders who hold a biblical worldview must be our guides. We need advocates who have a deep respect for life and a commitment to improve our culture, not diminish it.

As I've said often in this book, *you* are that advocate. The first handicapped people to be carted off by Nazi medical teams were disabled people who had no advocates, no one to speak up or stand up for them. When Psalm 140:12 states, "I know that the LORD secures justice for the poor and upholds the cause of the needy," God is thinking of *your* hands and *your* voice.

What Does It Involve?

Promote a pro-life perspective in your church by forming a disability ministry ... creating an outreach into nursing homes ... forming a partnership with your local Crisis Pregnancy Center.

Alert your church's prayer team on the need to cover these issues in prayer. Provide them with information on local, state, and national legislation or policies. If your church does not have a prayer team, organize a group of like-hearted Christians who will agree to bring these issues before the Lord in prayer.

Ask your pastor to address stem cell research in a sermon series, or to include it in Sanctity of Life Sunday.

Organize a panel discussion on stem cell research at your church.

Ask a Bible college or seminary in your community to hold an off-campus bioethics course at your church, then invite other churches to participate and advertise the course.

Ask an informed and interested couple in your church to host a short informational seminar on the ethics of artificial reproductive technologies, including in vitro fertilization.

Plan a Sunday school class using curriculum such as *Playing God?: Facing the Everyday Ethical Dilemmas of Biotechnology* by Charles Colson and Nigel Cameron, PhD (other curriculum resources are listed in our resources chapter).

Volunteer as an ombudsman at your local nursing home.

Ask how you, or an interested elder in your church, might serve on an ethics committee at your local hospital.

Sponsor a symposium at your church; gather four or five presenters who can speak to the topics in this book. To locate presenters in your area, contact the Center for Bioethics and Human Dignity.

Create a small watchdog task force that will investigate bills and initiatives in either your state assembly or in the US Congress. Contact your state representative of National Right to Life or go online to any of the organizations mentioned in our information and resources chapter.

Contact your state or US representatives at their district offices; leverage your vote by also asking a couple of friends to call or write. Follow up the effort by writing or calling your representatives at your state capital or in Washington, DC.

Coordinate a letter-writing party to reach your state or national representatives and local or state supreme court justices. These letters ought to be personal and not sound as though you copied them from an organized campaign. A personal letter informs not only legislators and judges, but their clerks and staff who do much of the research for the judicial or representative's office.

Connect with groups like Not Dead Yet or ADAPT to find out what policies or laws are encroaching on the welfare of disabled or elderly people (contact information for these and other groups is in our resources chapter).

Coordinate a network of writers who are either disabled or elderly to submit op-ed pieces and letters to editors, most especially newspapers in your state capital or Washington, DC.

Most of all, share your convictions in thoughtful, reasoned conversations with friends, neighbors, coworkers, and family members. To be salt and light in your community is to engage people in these issues, whether waiting in a hair salon, writing a letter to the editor, walking through a nursing home, talking in the coffee klatch, meeting on a community bioethics board in a hospital, sitting in the student lounge at college, or spending hours in an emergency room.

You are in a battle for the minds and hearts of men ... *you are the advocate.*

By the way, remember how we began this book hearing about Larry, the truck driver who broke his neck? The man who wanted so much to die? I thought you'd be interested to see what I wrote him ...

Dear Larry,

I can appreciate the fact that you just don't want to go on. Really. There are days when I wake up, even now, after all these years, and think, Lord Jesus, I don't have the strength. But the weaker I am physically, the harder I have to lean on the Lord; and the harder I lean on him, the stronger I discover him to be. God always seems bigger to those who need him most. He is drawn to people like you and me. He's attracted — he has a special heart for — the weak. And I will tell you flat out, I would rather be in my chair knowing him, than on my feet without him. I'm going to be praying for you over the next few weeks, asking God to aid and comfort you ... and that the Lord Jesus, the Bread of Life, the Resurrection and the Life, he who has the Words of Life will help you want to live. In the meantime, I'm sending you some resources and groups in your area who can serve as your advocate there in the nursing home.

Larry is *not* better off dead than disabled. The fact is, better to be disabled than follow the wisdom of this age. Better to follow life ... the Resurrection and the Life. And the life that Jesus gives is always abundant. It's why Jesus was nailed to the cross. Not only to redeem us from sin, but to reclaim this world as rightfully his.

That's the message that'll change Larry's heart. And it's the message that, with a lot of prayer, will change the soul of a society ... the heart of our nation.

JONI

CHAPTER 13

QUESTIONS PEOPLE ASK

You probably came to this book with questions, and having read it, still do not feel quite sure of the answers. Or perhaps you are just browsing and want something clear and quick. The following highlights some questions people have asked us, as well as a few of our short answers.

But bear in mind that short answers are never the full answer. What we have tried to do in *How to Be a Christian in a Brave New World* is to provide some context. This is all about getting a grasp on the big questions at stake in all the small questions: the big issues of eugenics, suffering, our power to design others and ourselves, and God's purposes for people.

So don't feel satisfied with these quick answers. Put them in the context of the stories and the arguments of the book. And then move on; use the resources in the next chapter. Get the *Playing God* Sunday school kit for your church. Explore the websites. And then you will move into a good position to get your own answers—and to give answers to others. We want you to join us in teaching the church how to live for God in the special world of the twenty-first century!

"DOES A CLONE HAVE A SOUL?"

Yes, of course! God doesn't give souls to some people and not to others. Genesis 1 says that *every* human being, every member of our species, is made in God's image. That means they have souls. We have souls from the moment we become human (which is when our biological lives start, as fertilized embryos or cloned embryos).

The fact that bad things were done to begin the lives of cloned people does not affect their status as people. Never doubt that even tiny embryos are fully human. Not only are they members of the human species (just like chimpanzee embryos are members of the chimp species), but we know that Jesus took human form as a zygote, a tiny embryo. That's when his human life began, and it's also when ours do.

If one day cloned babies are born, they too will be totally human, even if they resulted from the kind of planning and manufacturing that should never be used to make people. "Designed" humans are still human; but to the extent that they result from someone's planning, their human dignity is compromised.

Sometimes people say, "But the cloned baby is not unique; he or she is a copy." In genetics terms, that's true. But so are identical twins! Twins happen naturally, so there is nothing wrong with being a twin. Clones happen unnaturally, and of course instead of twins or triplets, you could have ten thousand "identical clones," all different ages, copies of a celebrity profiled in *People* magazine.

But genes are not everything. Even in the womb, twins become different in important ways: they have different fingerprints; their brains form in different ways. So the identical twins we know (and perhaps you are a twin!) are often similar in uncanny ways, but also different — sometimes very much so.

"WHAT CAN WE DO?"

People often ask this question with a sense of resignation, feeling that bad things are inevitable and that our efforts will go nowhere. That's not true!

Christians have made a huge difference in history precisely because they were not defeatists. They believed in a great God! And they could see opportunities all around them to make a difference.

Whether you make a difference in one person's life, or the nation's life, it's a huge difference. We can see today the impact Christians have made at high levels in politics. We can also see the difference they have made at ground level. The pro-life movement early on learned that we can do both, must do both — so we have Crisis Pregnancy Centers and we lobby Congress to push through laws to end "partial-birth abortion" and defend the unborn victims of violence.

We need exactly the same approach on these wider issues as we have taken on abortion. We need to live distinctive lives, to testify to our friends and neighbors and coworkers, and to work to defeat evil and promote what is good at every level in the culture. If we get discouraged, we need to remember the great example of William Wilberforce and his lifelong campaign to abolish slavery. And we also need to get better informed, because whatever discouragements we meet, there are always other places where things are going better. The media will not always help. Not many Americans know that "therapeutic cloning," such a huge issue in US politics, has actually been banned north of the border in Canada.

So there is something *everyone* can do! You need to think and pray and work out what it is for you.

"Should We Use In Vitro Fertilization?"

Christians take different stances on that question, and we can understand why. Catholics have been taught to avoid in vitro since it involves too many moral problems. Evangelicals often haven't thought about it at all. Some who have, agree that it is wrong. Others conclude that it all depends what you are doing with the technology. It's ultimately a question of conscience – making up your mind in the Lord's presence, after you have studied the pros and cons.

But some things seem clear to us. This is *not* a routine medical procedure; it is filled with moral problems. We don't think you should select the "best" embryos and discard the others. We don't think you should create more embryos than you are going to implant, nor that you should implant more than can be safely carried to term if they survive. We don't think it is ever right to freeze embryos; they are human beings, and pro-lifers do not stick other human beings in the freezer. We don't think that unmarried women should ever use in vitro; babies should be conceived in the context of marriage. We don't think surrogate mothering is ever justified; carrying someone else's baby for them, either for money (a womb-for-rent) or even for friends and family. And, of course, we don't think that "donor gametes" should be used – sperm and eggs from people other than the couple concerned.

Some people use in vitro to have their own babies, carefully restricting the use of the technology so that these evils can be avoided. Whether you do so is up to you, once you have prayed it through and talked it through and read all you can on the pros and cons of having a test-tube baby.

"WE HAVE USED IN VITRO AND WE HAVE FROZEN EMBRYOS; WHAT SHOULD WE DO NOW?"

You know the story of the traveler in Ireland who asked the way to Dublin? He was told: "You can't start from here!" In a fallen world, we always have to deal with situations we wish we had not gotten ourselves into.

The key is to remember *who* your frozen embryos are. They are not things; they are not part of your body; they are people: tiny, unconscious, frozen people. So what should you do? You should give them every chance of life. That will usually mean taking responsibility for having them implanted, and carrying them to term, if you are (medically) able to do that, as with every baby. It may be possible for them to be "adopted" by another couple, and programs like Snowflakes help make that possible. Using a "surrogate" mother to rescue an embryo who would otherwise perish is of course completely different from deliberately setting out to use in vitro for surrogate mothering—as different as adopting an orphan is from kidnapping or buying a baby.

"ARE TINY EMBRYOS REALLY HUMAN?"

When the press quotes pro-lifers, they often suggest that our beliefs are simply incredible. How can a tiny, microscopic embryo really have the kind of human dignity that brings the "right to life"? How can it be a he or a she, "one of us"?

When you put it like that, it *can* sound incredible. Early embryos—zygotes, blastocysts, various technical words describe them at different stages—are tiny, they are unconscious, they have no organs or nervous system or brain—and since the 1970s they have been available for experimentation. Some Christians who are definitely against abortion have their doubts. In fact, one of the most disheartening experiences in the debates about cloning and embryo stem cell research has been that some "anti-abortion" politicians have decided to trim their sails and come out in favor of destroying early embryos.

There are two basic answers to the question. One comes simply from science. While tiny embryos appear to us to be very different even from later embryos and fetuses (we use that word from eight weeks of gestation onwards), the problem lies with us. Our imagination is at fault. Every fact we have learned about genetics and embryology suggests that we are wrong to harbor these doubts. All it takes to turn an embryo into a college student is two things: a suitable environment, and food. So when someone says, "That doesn't look like a human being to me," the answer is, "That's exactly what human beings look like when they are young; it's what you and I looked like too at that age." A famous philosopher once wrote an essay with the title, "Was I a Zygote?" The answer, of course, is yes!

Many, many big shifts in human development turn a zygote into a voter. Some people have suggested that the biggest ones come after birth, when the new human being becomes self-aware and able to communicate, or when he or she becomes able to take care of himself or herself (teens? after college?). The point is that we are biological

Dr. Seuss's Answer

As to denigrating the worth of nascent human beings because of their size, the beloved Dr. Seuss story *Horton Hears a Who* offers a wonderful antidote:

> *Then he heard it again! Just a very faint yelp*
> *As if some tiny person were calling for help.*
> *… some poor little person who's shaking with fear*
> *That he'll blow in the pool! He has no way to steer!*
> *I'll just have to save him. Because, after all,*
> *A person's a person, no matter how small.*

beings who go through many changes. Unless we focus on what is special about the human species, we leave ourselves open to racism and other kinds of discrimination against the handicapped, the elderly, and whatever group of humans it becomes fashionable to regard as less than human.

But Christians have another answer. For us, it's easy! We believe in Jesus. And we know that Jesus became one of us in the incarnation. As soon as his mother Mary conceived him, miraculously, by the power of the Holy Spirit, his human life as the Son of God began. Read the Christmas story at the start of Luke's gospel, and remember that Luke was a physician. He tells how when Mary was only a few weeks pregnant, she met her cousin Elizabeth, six months pregnant with John the Baptist. John "leaped" for joy in Elizabeth's womb at the presence of the tiny Jesus in Mary's, giving his first testimony to Jesus. And, of course, we read in Genesis 1 that every member of the species is made in the image of God. That's how Jesus could take human nature, because we are already made in God's image. And it's how he could become incarnate as a zygote.

"Shouldn't Christians Be in Favor of Cures?"

The embryo research debate has sometimes degenerated into a shouting match — at least, from the other side. However reasonable we try to be, we get shouted at. We try to make a reasoned case about the need for ethical science, about the dangers of mass-producing humans for experiments, about the fact that science has in the past done terrible things (remember Nazi Germany). They yell back: "We can get cures!" It can be a strange thing to be a Christian in public debate today; we are always accused of being irrational, but we are the ones with the reasoned case!

Of course we favor "cures." We may be skeptical of hype, and there never has been hype like the extravagant and often very dishonest language used by scientists and biotech lobbyists in their search for federal money and their desire to avoid any kind of ethical regulation on what they do. We favor cures that come from ethical research.

And the wonderful thing about recent discoveries in the life sciences is that there are many possible ways of coming to the same results. Not many people know that *all* of the applications of "stem cell research" to human beings have not come from using embryos at all, but what are called "adult" stem cells—the cells hidden away in your own body! Check out the websites we list in the next chapter for the latest details.

"I'm a Pastor, and I Am Concerned That Our Church Not Get into Politics."

We agree! Churches are not meant to be party affiliated, and only rarely should they get into anything on the political agenda. Christians come to different decisions on issues of party politics, and our churches need to remain places where you are free to be Democrat, Republican, or to join smaller parties that uphold human dignity and freedom. Catholics have tended to be more Democrat (though the abortion issue has been pushing many of them to vote for the GOP). White evangelicals tend to vote Republican. African American evangelicals tend to vote Democrat. We make our political decisions for many reasons, and it's important that pastors and teachers in the churches don't tell us, "If you are a real Christian, you need to vote for X."

At the same time, churches need to teach the values of Christian living for the twenty-first century. They should not tell us how to vote, but they do need to tell us that we *should* vote and get well-informed about the issues behind elections. Sometimes there will be a big single-issue campaign (like the ballot initiatives in California on euthanasia and embryonic stem cell research) on which Christians have a very distinctive view, not party political. This may happen on a local issue, such as a plan for gambling. The church does not suddenly become "political," but it needs to give a lead so that its members feel encouraged to act as Christian citizens, have the best information, and feel confident that it's right for believers to take a lead in the culture and campaign for good things and against evil ones. That is what being "salt and light" in a democracy is all about.

Many Christians think only two options exist: turn the church into a political campaigning group; or opt out entirely and live as if you were on the moon. Neither of these is the Christian way. A key task of the church is to educate believers to become informed citizens and to exercise their citizenship for Jesus Christ. That will never be more important than in the brave new world.

RESPOURCES TO LIVE IN

THE BRAVE NEW WORLD

In this appendix we'd like to suggest how you can "go deeper" on this issue by taking advantage of several kinds of resources:

1. Curriculum and books
2. Magazines, websites, and organizations
3. Academic programs
4. Sources of information from the book's chapters

We have introduced you to the main points of discussion as they currently exist; now you can become better informed and more effective in your response by becoming acquainted with some of the excellent materials available to you.

1. CURRICULUM AND BOOKS

Sunday School/Small Group Curriculum:

Colson, Charles and Nigel M. de S. Cameron, *Playing God* (Loveland, Colo.: Group, 2004). This curriculum features Colson and Cameron in video and audio clips, together with biology professor David Prentice, in twelve weekly segments. This is an ideal package for churches and does not need an expert to lead the group; leader and student guides are provided. Details at *www.grouppublishing.com.*

Books from a Christian Viewpoint:

These books are accessible to people who do not know much about the subject. Read them all and you will be on your way to becoming an expert.

Bevington, Linda, et al., *Basic Questions on Genetics, Stem Cell Research, and Cloning* (Grand Rapids, Mich.: Kregel, 2004) – very useful introduction in the form of Q and A.

Cameron, Nigel M. de S., *The New Medicine: Life and Death after Hippocrates* (Chicago: Bioethics Press, 2002) – an overview of the challenges facing medicine with the collapse of the sanctity of life; includes an appendix on the theology of healing.

Colson, Charles and Nigel M. de S. Cameron, eds., *Human Dignity in the Biotech Century* (Westmont, Ill.: InterVarsity, 2004), includes chapters on many of the issues we discuss in this book, written by experts in science, law, policy, and other fields. This is not an "academic" book; it is meant for Christians who want to learn more of what is happening and how we should respond. It's the perfect next step after *How to Be a Christian in a Brave New World*.

Kilner, John F. and C. Ben Mitchell, *Does God Need Our Help? Cloning, Assisted Suicide, and Other Challenges in Bioethics* (Wheaton, Ill.: Tyndale, 2003)—highly recommended overview of key bioethics issues.

Stewart, Gary, et al., *Basic Questions on Sexuality and Reproductive Technology* (Grand Rapids, Mich.: Kregel, 1998)—another in the Basic Questions series.

Tada, Joni Eareckson, *When Is It Right to Die? Euthanasia on Trial* (New York: HarperCollins, 1993)—a powerful case against the push for "assisted suicide" and euthanasia. We thought about including a chapter on euthanasia in this book, but decided against it so we could focus more on the new technologies. But the old issues are not going away, and "euthanasia" has a lot in common with "eugenics." They are both made-up words, and mean "good death" and "good genes" or "good life." Yet what they really mean is death designed by choice, and life designed by choice—*our* choice, not God's.

Books That May Be Harder to Read, Some by Christians:

These are books that a newcomer to the biotech field might like to read.

Andrews, Lori B., *Future Perfect: Confronting Decisions about Genetics* (New York: Columbia University Press, 2001)—Lori Andrews is widely seen as the leading US expert on biotech law and is a liberal feminist, but on these new issues we tend to agree with her. Readable and very informative.

Black, Edwin, *War Against the Weak: Eugenics and America's Campaign to Create a Master Race* (New York: Four Walls Eight Windows, 2003)—powerful and very readable book that tells the story of American eugenics and its relationship to the Nazis.

Fukuyama, Francis, *Our Posthuman Future: Consequences of the Biotechnology Revolution* (New York: Picador, 2002) – as the title says, explores the consequences of our new biotech knowledge. Fukuyama is a major intellectual and the book is not all easy going. But we welcome many of his conclusions.

Kristol, William and Eric Cohen, eds., *The Future Is Now: America Confronts the New Genetics* (Lanham, Md.: Rowman and Littlefield, 2002) – helpful collection of mainly recent essays, speeches, and testimony on the biotech agenda. Kristol is editor of the conservative *Weekly Standard.*

Meilaender, Gilbert, *Bioethics: A Primer for Christians* (Grand Rapids, Mich.: Eerdmans, 1996) – very readable, short book by a philosopher who is also a member of the President's Council on Bioethics.

Moravec, Hans, *Robot: Mere Machine to Transcendent Mind* (New York: Oxford, 1999) – a very positive book about artificial intelligence by a guru in the world of robotics.

Rifkin, Jeremy, *The Biotech Century: Harnessing the Gene and Remaking the World* (New York: Putnam, 1998) – Rifkin is a global leader of the environmental movement, and this book helped popularize the term "biotech century." A brilliant book that surveys developments in human biotech and also agricultural biotech. Rifkin is very skeptical of humans' capacity to use their new powers responsibly.

Silver, Lee M., *Remaking Eden: Cloning and Beyond in a Brave New World* (New York: Avon Books, 1998) – Silver is a biology professor and writes with enthusiasm about the amazing possibilities of the brave new world, which he welcomes. Despite the title (and many Bible quotes), he is not a Christian.

2. Magazines, Websites, and Organizations

The magazine *Ethics and Medicine* is published three times a year and offers unique Christian perspectives on the bioethics/biotech debates. Both the Center for Bioethics and Human Dignity and the Center for Bioethics and Culture include *Ethics and Medicine* in membership packages. You can subscribe direct at *www.ethicsandmedicine.com.*

A journal called *The New Atlantis* is now published by the Ethics and Public Policy Center in Washington, DC. It broadly surveys issues of science and technology, though with a special focus on the biotech agenda. You can subscribe at *www.thenewatlantis.com*.

The Center for Bioethics and Culture is a Christian network with centers in several states that help educate nonspecialists. Its website (*www. thecbc.org*) has excellent resources, and the free email newsletter carries updates.

The Center for Bioethics and Human Dignity, based in Deerfield, Illinois, has a well-stocked website (*www.cbhd.org*) and networks physicians and others. It includes a list of speakers. We have both spoken more than once at its summer conference.

The Wilberforce Forum's Council for Biotechnology Policy has a website at *www.biotechpolicy.org*, and emails a monthly biotech update newsletter.

Go to *www.joniandfriends.org* for key material on biotech issues, especially in relation to disability and the stem cell research debate.

Two key websites that carry basic news and information on their respective subjects are:

www.stemcellresearch.org
www.cloninginformation.org

The Institute on Biotechnology and the Human Future, based at Chicago-Kent College of Law in the Illinois Institute of Technology, brings together Christians and secularists, conservatives and progressives, in addressing the challenges of biotechnology. See *www.thehumanfuture.org*.

The Christian Medical and Dental Association (*www.cmdahome.org*) is a network for Christian physicians.

Other groups that include some biotech related materials on their websites are:

National Right to Life Committee (*www.nrlc.org*)
Family Research Council (*www.frc.org*)
Concerned Women for America (*www.cwfa.org*)
Focus on the Family (*www.fotf.org*)

The website of the President's Council on Bioethics in Washington, DC, has downloadable copies of key reports by the Council which contain important material (*www.bioethics.gov*).

When it comes to disability-related issues and how they impact Americans with disabilities, our friends at Not Dead Yet stand on the front lines in safeguarding the most vulnerable among us. Whether it's writing a friend of the court brief or organizing a quiet protest in front of the Supreme Court, you will find NDY members in their wheelchairs, protecting the rights of the medically fragile.

Not Dead Yet
c/o Progress CIL
7521 Madison St
Forest Park, IL 60130
Phone: 708-209-1500
www.notdeadyet.org

The American Association of People with Disabilities is the largest nonprofit cross-disability member organization in the US, dedicated to ensuring political empowerment for the more than 56 million Americans with disabilities. AAPD works in coalition with other disability organizations for the full implementation and enforcement of disability non-discrimination laws. The AAPD website has a subscriber news service entitled *Justice for All*, which provides current action alerts and news items which pertain to the rights of people with disabilities.

AAPD
1629 K Street NW, Suite 503
Washington, DC 20006
Phone: 800-840-8844 (toll free, V/TTY)
www.aapd-dc.org

It is an unfortunate reality that many people with disabilities and their families feel disenfranchised from church life or even the Christian faith. The HumanLifeMatters ministry was established to lift up their innate value and dignity within a church family, under the lordship of Jesus Christ. HumanLifeMatters (HLM) exists to help local churches develop meaningful ministries of inclusion to make people impacted by disabilities indispensable members of their congregations and society. Human-LifeMatters will provide speakers and workshops related to areas such as:

- Sanctity of human life and disability
- Disability and your congregation
- Loss, suffering, and Christian growth

HumanLifeMatters
4417–51 Street

Beaumont, AB
Canada
T4X 1C8
Phone: 780-929-9231
www.humanlifematters.com

Christian Life Resources (CLR) has been serving people since 1983 with information and support on life and family issues. Using God's Word as the motivation, they develop materials and services to guide people in making ethical decisions that are in accordance with Scripture.

Available to you through CLR are books and videos from their extensive lending library, a comprehensive website, brochures, videos, and books that cover timely and difficult topics, and a caring staff willing to help.

Christian Life Resources
2949 N. Mayfair Road, Suite 309
Milwaukee, WI 53222-4304
Phone: 414-774-1331
www.christianliferesources.com

3. Academic Programs

Two Christian schools now offer graduate programs for those who want to know more – whether you are an MD or a lawyer or a student considering moving into the bioethics field. Other schools offer individual courses.

Covenant Theological Seminary in Saint Louis has begun offering a graduate certificate in bioethics.

Trinity International University in Deerfield, Illinois, has since the mid-1990s offered a master's program in bioethics.

Both of these schools make it possible to complete their programs without moving to campus for long periods; courses are bundled around weekends and into short summer modules, and some can be taken at a distance. Both these programs are cosponsored by bioethics centers. The Center for Bioethics and Human Dignity on Trinity's campus also offers a weeklong summer "institute" program for those who want a taste of serious study without plunging into a new degree. The Covenant program is cosponsored by the St. Louis Center for Bioethics and Culture.

Get more details from the websites: *www.covenantsem.edu* and *www. tiu.edu.*

4. Sources of Information from the Book's Chapters

References and further sources for each of the chapters are as follows:

Chapter 2

The idea for the section discussing the Larry King interview came from *National Review Online,* "The Wrong Cure" by Wesley J. Smith, September 9, 2004. The letter from progressive leaders seeking a cloning moratorium can be found on the website of the Center for Genetics and Society, *www.genetics-and-society.org.* The Council for Responsible Genetics has a website at *www.crg.org.*

Chapter 4

Edwin Black's statement about the "Eugenics Record Office" and his discussion of California sterilization are quoted from an article he wrote in the *San Francisco Chronicle* on November 9, 2003. His description of the raid on the Virginia hill people is from his book *War Against the Weak,* pages 3 – 4 (New York: Four Walls Eight Windows, 2003). Sources for the story of Carrie Buck include the Eugenics Archive (*www.eugenicsarchive.org*) and Elof A. Carlson, *The Unfit: The History of a Bad Idea* (Cold Spring Harbor, N.Y.: Cold Spring Harbor Laboratory Press, 2001). See also: P. A. Lombardo, "Three Generations, No Imbeciles: New Light on Buck v. Bell." *New York University Law Review* 60 (1985): 30 – 62. Christine Rosen's fine book, *Preaching Eugenics,* was published in 2004 by Oxford University Press. For information and hundreds of pictures from the American eugenics movement see *www.eugenicsarchive.org/eugenics.*

Chapter 5

The study on the risks of birth defects is: "The Risk of Major Birth Defects After Intercytoplasmic Sperm Injection and In Vitro Fertilization," *New England Journal of Medicine,* March 7, 2002. The article in *Time* on the same subject has the interesting title: "The Limits of Science," April 15, 2002. Arthur Caplan's revealing quote is from Maria Gallagher, *www.LifeNews.com,* September 1, 2004. News of the disability lobby of the United Nations is from the Friday Fax for May 28, 2004, of C-FAM. The story of Karen Coveler's genetic tests is from the *New York Times* of July 21, 2004. The *Times* report on how much of an abnormality should be grounds for abortion is from June 20, 2004. The *Journal of the American Medical Association*'s commentary on the ethics of pre-implantation diagnosis was published on June 27, 2001 (285:24).

Chapter 6

The report on "Copy Cat" is from *Nature* online for February 14, 2002. The reporter's comment on the Raelian hoax is from the *Independent*, a national daily based in London, December 28, 2002. Dr. Richard Seed is quoted from a CNN interview on July 26, 1998. Arnold Schwarzenegger was interviewed on *Extra TV* on November 15, 2000; quote at *www.humancloning.org*. Baroness Warnock was interviewed in the UK's *Herald* newspaper on July 26, 2002. The American Society for Reproductive Medicine's website gives their position: *www.ASRM.org*. Dr. Jaenisch was speaking to the *Ottawa Citizen*, September 11, 2002, and the spokesperson for the Humane Society to US Newswire on August 13, 2002. The couple who told Connie Chung that God had approved their cloning are quoted in the *New York Daily News* for August 11, 2002. The quote from Nobel laureate James Watson is from the UK's *Independent on Sunday*, April 13, 2003. The wonderful epitaph for Dolly the sheep was written by Reuters, April 9, 2002.

Chapter 7

The sad story of Sharla Miller's search for a daughter is quoted from the *Orlando Sentinel* for July 14, 2004. Laura Howard's surprise was reported by the Associated Press on July 15, 2004. The assessment of China's missing babies is by Joseph A. D'Agostino in the Population Research Institute's Weekly Briefing, February 7, 2005. The warning from the chair of the UK's Human Genetics Commission comes from the *Financial Times* for July 16, 2004, and the report of concerns from the Human Fertilisation and Embryology Authority from the *Gulf Daily News*, July 18, 2004. The report on "our biotech bodies" is taken from *US News and World Report* for May 31, 2004. The statement from Pope John Paul II is from his encyclical *Evangelium Vitae* (The Gospel of Life), March 25, 1995. The full text of the PBS *Frontline* interview is at *www.pbs.org/wgbh/pages/frontline/shows/fertility/interviews/cameron.html*. Kate's decision to abort her child with Down syndrome is an example of a much wider problem that is being recognized even in places like the *New York Times*, "In New Tests for Fetal Defects, Agonizing Choices" by Amy Harmon; June 20, 2004.

Chapter 8

Dr. James Dobson's comments were quoted at *www.Family.org*, on June 28, 2004; Steve Milloy's at *www.Foxnews.com*, on July 16, 2004. Rebecca Griffin sent Nigel Cameron a copy of her remarkable statement, which was then quoted in part by Charles W. Colson on a *Breakpoint* broadcast. The amazing stem cell story is from the *Korea Times* for December 3, 2004. Yet South Korea persists in its desire to do "therapeutic cloning"!

Chapter 9

Tara Schupner quotes the Dutch doctor in an article on *www.Kansan.com*, November 16, 2004. Tara is deaf. The ban on insurance company testing in the UK was reported by the *Sydney Morning Herald*, November 5, 2004. President Clinton's speech about genetic discrimination was made on February 8, 2000. Testimony before Senator Gregg's committee was reported by Reuters on July 22, 2004. The report on Doris Goldman's family in the *San Jose Mercury News* was published on December 6, 2000. Hillary August's article, "Facing Genetic Discrimination First Hand," is in *Insight* 1 (2006) on "Genetic Discrimination," from the Institute on Biotechnology and the Human Future. The quotes from Christopher Hook, MD, of Mayo Clinic, and Professor Allen Verhey of Hope College, Michigan, are taken from: "When Does Personhood Begin?" by Bob Smietana in *Christianity Today* for July 2004, pages 26 and 28.

Chapter 10

Details of Lori Andrews's book, *Future Perfect*, are given previously in the recommended reading section. The report on the patenting of sick dogs was carried by the *Wall Street Journal* for May 28, 2004. The *Washington Post*'s report on super mice was published October 1, 2000, and its discussion of patenting and the 13th Amendment on May 17, 2002. The *New York Times* report on the European human patent confusion appeared on May 14, 2000. The full reference to the Weldon Amendment is: Consolidated Appropriations Act of 2004, Pub. L. No. 108–199, 118 Stat. 3, Division B, Title VI, Section 634 (2004). The BIO memo to congressional offices supporting the patenting of embryos was dated September 2, 2003. Richard Doerflinger's comment was quoted in a press release put out by the National Right to Life Committee on February 4, 2004. The *Wall Street Journal*'s far-sighted report was published on August 20, 2001. We are grateful to Amber Standridge for helping research this debate. Bob

Smietana's quote is from his article on "When Does Personhood Begin?" in *Christianity Today*, July 2004, page 24.

For the deaths of disabled children under the Nazis, see Shawna Parks, *New Mobility Magazine*, "The Legacy of Nazism," June 2001, page 86. For more information, visit the Disability Holocaust Project at *www.dralegal. org* or read *By Trust Betrayed: Patients, Physicians, and the License to Kill in the Third Reich* by Hugh Gregory Gallagher (Vandamere Press, 1995). For details on the medical team advocating nontreatment for babies with spina bifida, see Not Dead Yet facts, *www.notdeadyet.org*. The interview with Willard Gaylin is in *Harpers Magazine*, October 1993. (He is also featured in a quote at the start of the movie *Gattaca*.) The campaign by disability groups from right and left is reported in an interview with Stephen Drake, Research Analyst for Not Dead Yet, 7521 Madison Street, Forest Park, IL 60130, *www.notdeadyet.org*. Not Dead Yet is a vigorous disability rights group. Journalist Neil Munro was writing for *Washington Monthly* in November 2002.

Chapter 11

David Cohn's report was at Wired.com, October 26, 2004. Simon Collins's report about Kevin Warwick was in the *New Zealand Herald* for July 6, 2004. Selmer Bringsjord's article is in the *Chronicle of Higher Education*, November 3, 2000. Bill Joy's famed article has been reprinted in many places and is highly readable. It originally appeared as the cover article in *Wired* magazine for April 2000. The quote from James Hughes of the World Transhumanist Association was posted to a Listserv. The report *Converging Technologies for Improving Human Performance* was published in 2002 by the National Science Foundation, an agency of the US government. The story on Jim Wilson's monkeys is in the *Boston Globe* for November 2, 2004. *Science News* wrote on H. Lee Sweeney's work on October 30, 2004. John Piper's comment is quoted from "Brokenhearted Joy," *World Magazine*, December 13, 2003.

We want to hear from you. Please send your comments about this book to us in care of zreview@zondervan.com. Thank you.

ZONDERVAN™

GRAND RAPIDS, MICHIGAN 49530 USA

ZONDERVAN.COM/
AUTHOR**TRACKER**